America's Hope

COLIN ARMORGIE

Copyright © 2023 Colin Armorgie

All rights reserved.

ISBN: 978-1-3999-5875-2

In memory of my Dad,
who never knew.

CONTENTS

Acknowledgements	i
Lost	1
Disclaimers	7
Pithy quote	11
A beginning, a middle and an end	13
A journey into cliché territory	15
Why did I start?	19
Introducing Spero	23
One of the few	27
A-Day: The Armorgie Genesis	29
Stories of misspellings	31
Spero becomes the destination	37
Digression	39
The Armorgie sagas	41
Inheriting things that matter	45
Why *was* I going to Bath?	47
Self-help	53
I was unprepared	59
The sins of our fathers	63
Serendipitous beginnings	69
The opening ceremony	75
The making of a scouser	79

Epiphany	91
What was I looking for?	97
Who? What? Where? When? Why?	101
Route 1 – DNA Brothers	105
Route 2 – Blood Brothers	111
The walls have ears	117
Realisation	121
Burdens	123
Leamington Spa	129
Norman Stewart Walker	137
It won't happen to me	141
Inference-observation confusion	145
Trusting to luck is not a strategy	147
Probability of success	153
"Suspicion often creates what it suspects"	155
Two's company, three's a crowd	159
Paternity Suit #1: A load of Bullochs?	163
America's Hope?	167
In the town where I was born lived a man who sailed to sea	171
Paternity Suit #2: Skip to my Lou(isa)	175
Caught up in the double helix	179
Evidence from the history of American settlement	183
Breakthrough!	185

Respice finem	191
Mano a mano	195
Maverick and Iceman	199
The sleep of swords	201
Poacher turned gamekeeper	203
Not a lot of people know this	207
Has anyone seen Spero?	211
Things start to go south from here	213
How much further south is this going?	215
Me llamo Hunter Davidson	217
Here is where I rest my case	221
The Gowan connection	223
The Cheryl Piccola-Sullivan connection	227
The Pablo Tabachnik connection	229
An uncomfortable truth	231
A big fat middle, two ends and several beginnings	235
Pithy quotes reconsidered	237
What has all this given me?	239
Tying up loose threads	243
The final chapter or the next chapter?	245
References	247
About the author	248

ACKNOWLEDGEMENTS

I am indebted to Tamsin Pollentine, whose passion for writing gave me the *cojones* to write my story, so blame her. Thanks also inevitably go to a number of people who share my surname - my brothers Paul, Roger, Neil, and the fifth Beatle, my cousin Phil. They all similarly provided great encouragement as well providing stories from our lives and not objecting when I changed their version of events to fit my narrative. The lesson is, blokes, if you want it told your way, write your own bloody book. Additionally, I am grateful to another cousin, Peter Blaney, who has Armorgie blood running through his veins to dilute the South African red wine. Peter knew more Armorgie history than anyone else.

Finally, but most significant, thanks alone are not enough to cover the contribution of Shelley Armorgie, who helped with the editing but more so with the research and looking interested when I told her every minute detail of what I found. Also, her family history of opium runners makes me feel less bad about the potentially embarrassing bits in Armorgie history.

LOST

I was lost. Not lost-lost, not proper David Livingstone lost, just lost in terms of I couldn't be bothered to use a map and compass to work out where I was. So I was just lazy-lost really, and those in possession of an education in the history of navigation, or old age as it is otherwise referred to, will realise that I am not talking about more modern times.

Admittedly, being lost in the olden-days did involve a sort of GPS, but back then it was just a business management bullshit acronym that stood for Goals Plans Success. With the benefit of now being in possession of 20:20 hindsight, I look back and wish I had actually paid attention to some managers in those early days of my career, but I was blessed with KIA, a concept of which my manager was blissfully unaware: Knowing It All. Knowing It All trumps Goals Plans Success in all situations; I know this, I know all of this.

I headed straight for the Success part and skipped over the impediments of Goals and Plans. This involved me moving swiftly on, splitting an infinitive without a backwards glance whilst simultaneously embracing many a cliché. Success of a sort but still lost, nevertheless.

You may sense a theme already – me receiving advice and then ignoring it. But, hey, I haven't promised that this would be a self-help guide to navigating a way through life's little problems.

I know enough to say that staying positive is important when finding oneself lost. This I know because I've watched many personal survival documentaries on TV. I know that out of adversity comes a learning opportunity that can be applied to future problems, thus presenting a better chance of solving those problems. I didn't realise I felt that way until just now when I wrote that, or perhaps I am trying to mask the embarrassment of someone with a degree in geography who just got lost. Yes, I was lost then and I am getting increasingly lost in my story.

How to start? *Once upon a time* is a good start to many a good fabrication, so that feels appropriate.

Once upon a time, I was cycling in deepest rural England *en route* from London to Bath, on roads wonderfully less travelled, on a hot summer's day where even the birds seemed too relaxed to sing and the cows in the fields were lying in what little shade could be found. If it were today, I would probably take the cows' lead and opt for lying in the shade of a tree rather than riding a bike. I was young and foolish back then; now I am older. Note the full stop.

This was in those heady, carefree, distant days of my life when I wore a younger man's Lycra. The date is unimportant but it was in that window in history shortly after the wheel was invented and shortly before the internet was invented. My destination on that day, however, does have definite relevance - both in the context of this story and very much in my life. There is more of that to follow - in a good way. Trust me.

It was one of those timeless summer days where no one appeared to be in a particular hurry. That is possibly because there was no one but myself to be seen on this sun-dappled lane. The lane led me to a junction with another lane and a signpost told me that I had come from Wooton

AMERICA'S HOPE

Rivers and had a choice of going towards New Mill, Martinsell Hill or Clench Common. None of these names meant anything to me; in fact, the signpost was about as useful as a carpet fitter's ladder.

What is the best thing to do when lost? Of course, as in those personal survival documentaries, I should make a fire and a makeshift shelter, or if not that, I should at least stop and find my whereabouts. I cycled on. On rounding a corner I saw a man who was clearing a ditch at the side of the lane. His is a bit part in the story of my life but I will promote him to the role of Gentleman Farmer because, not only did he teach me a lesson but I feel that a grand title befits the person in an opening scene. I shall be less deferential as I proceed; which is a metaphor for my life. Remember, this man *is* sharing the scene with someone as illustrious as Dr David Livingstone, one of the most famous lost persons of all time, so the title of Gentleman Farmer feels somehow sufficiently respectful.

I had to do that most un-manly thing and stop to ask for directions. It's OK – no one was watching. One of the skills which I have been blessed with is the ability to be in a foreign country and to blunder with good intent. On such skills the British Empire was built. My children are kind enough not only to agree with my blundering skills but have been known, on occasions, to helpfully point this out. In this instance I was not in a foreign country but I might as well have been, so I employed my skill.

"Excuse me, which way is it to Bath, please?" I cautiously asked Gentleman Farmer, omitting the use of "my good man" as a form of address. Gentleman Farmer was in possession of various implements of potential destruction which possibly had something to do with my cautious approach.

"Barrf? Watcha wanna go thurr furr?" He responded in the dialect that placed him somewhere that shouldn't have been a mere 90 miles from the cut-glass tones heard further east in Buckingham Palace.

It was actually a good question, but if I deviated to answer it that would have placed Gentleman Farmer into the secondary role of the Priest Administering a Sacrament of Penance. It had its attraction, I have to admit; my state of being lost wouldn't be solved but I might end up feeling a whole lot better about myself. Not only a whole lot better, would it have meant that my reasons for going to Bath were instantly removed. That wouldn't work because it would also further spoil the flow of my story, if that's possible, or even end the story if you were lucky.

You are actually unlucky – carry on reading.

"I'm on a pilgrimage", I muttered whilst waving a hand like Obi-Wan Kenobi saying, "These are not the droids you're looking for."

Thinking about it now, pilgrimage was kind of true, as you will later see, and it kind of worked, as you will now see. The indication of it kind of having worked was established by a grunt. Was it down to my playing of the religion card or was it the Jedi dismissal?

"Barrf? Few gonna Barff, you dun wonna be sturrtun fr'meerr, may," he replied, sending my spell checker into meltdown.

Apparently, I didn't want to start my journey to Bath from that precise point in the middle of who-knows-where, mate. I can't fault the advice but to have told him it was utterly useless advice would have sounded ungrateful, so I tried a humorous literary allegory.

"I probably can't simply walk into Mordor, either – and if I tried, I probably wouldn't start from fucking Bag End."

Whoosh! I heard the sound of my arrow of literary wit missing the target. As it turns out, this was actually one of life's learning experiences. I found I could cycle quite quickly from a standing start when necessity required it. A quick start wasn't amongst the learning opportunities to which I earlier referred but I treated it as some sort of bonus. The real learning in this experience was the importance of knowing where to start a journey.

I should also have learned to use consistent examples when telling a story rather than flowing randomly from deepest Africa to Middle Earth, but that lesson has yet to sink in as will become apparent. Fluidity is kind of apt, however, given that this is a theme of what is to follow.

The good news here is that the flabby middle has been preceded by a flabby beginning, so I can tick off "beginning" on my list of how to write a book. Onwards!

DISCLAIMERS

What was that initial chapter all about?

I realise that having started my pilgrimage and getting lost, I ought to give some context so that you don't decide that watching interminable re-runs of *Friends* on TV is a preferable way to exercise your mind. Therefore, with no presumption that this story will ever make it into a book with a cover and some cover text or abstract describing the content, and no presumption that anyone would ever read such spin, I ought to say what this book is actually about. It is loosely about my family history; more specifically about why and how I discovered that history. The "why" is more important than the "how", as you will see.

To serve as some sort of hook to keep you reading, I have returned to insert this disclaimer, not only about my peculiar attempts at humour but also about some of the content which may be considered to be in some way contentious. Hey, if I could foresee my own faults, I probably wouldn't have started.

I had this realisation that a disclaimer was required after I got to the end of writing what, in all honesty, I never expected to end up writing when I started. See what I mean about getting lost? Yes, I know, your advice would be that I should have had a plan but it's too late for that now.

Moving swiftly on from that buffering in my stream of consciousness, I thought I ought to get in some sort of pre-emptory defence to add to the context of the story. That is a defence of both the rambling (but engaging) narrative and of my intention to mention people alive and dead, people fictional and nonfictional, and people who are not necessarily aware that they have been mentioned. Yet.

Let me start by being clear that this is all someone else's fault, not mine. I was told that I should write down what I had found about my family history because I had an interesting story to tell. It is definitely an interesting story but the test is whether I can tell it in an interesting way.

"You've got a way with words," was what I was told.

This was quite similar to experiences in my career where I wrote technical reports and always managed to "get away with words". This whole different meaning will be my defence if the libel lawyers come knocking.

What follows is a work of fact that contains some element of fiction, or possibly a work of fiction that contains some fact; it's a moot point. If you find the fiction, please don't let me know as there will be no prize and you will only risk being offended when you find that I am really not interested.

In this work of fictional fact, any resemblance of people who are referenced to actual persons, living or dead, or actual events, is absolutely and intentionally coincidental. That's the only way I could tell the story.

Additionally, as a warning, this work contains flashing images; flashing back to images of events and people that came before me and shaped who I am.

In the interests of aligning expectations, I think that a full appreciation of what is to follow can only be acquired with a sense of humour, ideally a British sense of humour. It is probably more than that, actually, in that the humour derives originally from a Liverpool heritage. I say "derives" as my heritage is Liverpudlian but I probably now qualify to be a fully paid-up, posh southerner – someone from the south of England; I will later elaborate on this.

While I am considering advance warnings, please be aware that I do not claim that this is a reliable history text book; appearances may be deceptive. In a book about family history it is impossible to avoid referencing "real" history and, indeed, I have a fascination for understanding the social, political and economic climate that my ancestors were part of. This is a bit like me stating that the aforementioned *Friends* was a documentary of New York life in the 1990s and early 2000s.

Having said that, and not going too deeply into an academic minefield, it is very unclear what defines "reliable history". The judgement of what is reliable is whatever I can get you to believe.

Even if I take out the reliability element of my telling of my family history, I like the idea of the problem that will be posed for anyone who has to categorise books. Fiction or non-fiction? History or historical fiction? Self-help or helplessly selfish?

Given the potential international interest that there may be in this story, I was hoping to help readers with the peculiar humour. Strangely though, I could find no online humor translator (see what I did there?) to supplement all the other Really Useful Stuff that I have found online to enable this story to effectively tell itself.

Finally, I hope that the humour will be understood and appreciated, even by the lawyers whose clients may have requested them to read this.

PITHY QUOTE

When I started to write about my research into my family name and family history, I thought I would try and be all arty and professional, and start with a pithy quote from someone famous. Well, I have failed in that endeavour, haven't I, in as much as I didn't start with any quote? You will learn that what I am about to tell you doesn't flow in a linear, chronological narrative; that would be too easy for you.

Those of you of a certain vintage may remember an apt quote, and excuse me for mashing it up, that this story is all the right memories, just not necessarily in the right order.

I could find many similar quotes that would make a good start, too many, but I couldn't find just one that I agreed with as reflecting exactly how I felt at that time. That is probably more down to my feelings changing rather than there not being any quotes.

On the other hand, maybe I could get inspiration from a quote? No. One thing I have not lacked in investigating my family's past is inspiration. Quotes on history are mainly about learning lessons and using it to shape the future. That's not what I wanted to do. If there are any lessons to be learned, they are lessons about determination and the reward that can come from unexpected sources – and how not to tell a story.

COLIN ARMORGIE

Fear not about the absence of a pithy quote here as I have sprinkled so many aphorisms throughout the rest of this book you will end up significantly pithed off. Here we go...

"I have only made this story longer because I have not had the time to make it shorter."

"The lovers of truth can go elsewhere for satisfaction but where can the lovers of romance turn if not to history?"

These are just two misquotes that have come close to describing what follows and, at the risk of sounding a little conceited, but nevertheless genuine, if there is anything in what I have written that inspires others to simultaneously dig deep into their past and into their heart, then please take it.

A BEGINNING, A MIDDLE AND AN END

Having gathered a lot of details about my family history, some reliable and some of another sort, I wanted to arrange what I had found into something ordered and coherent. Hard as it is to believe, I followed that ambition and this is the result.

My understanding was always that a story had to simply have a beginning, a middle and an end. Having started this story, I'm thinking that 2 out of 3 wouldn't be bad. I'll settle for 1 - the middle, and not unlike a middle-aged man, rather flabby and bloated. I'm not selling this very well but bear with me while I explain - "explain" being a euphemism for "make excuses".

Here's the problem; if I were to tell the family history story in chronological order that would make it logical and easy to follow. The problem with that is that I don't see how a story about family history can have a single start point. Two parents, four grandparents, eight great grandparents... you see the problem.

Even when I decided to tell just the story of my paternal lineage, it was difficult. How far back am I expected to go? The Olduvai Gorge? Possibly man's descent from the apes? Life leaving the oceans and first crawling upon the land?

COLIN ARMORGIE

Single-celled critters in a primordial soup? The Big Bang? You see the problem - I can't really promise a totally chronological beginning without this story becoming a history of life on Earth.

Maybe in my next book if David Attenborough doesn't beat me to it.

A JOURNEY INTO CLICHÉ TERRITORY

I realise that I have made reference to something of a journey, which has become the go-to cliché for those describing their life, or learning something, or, particularly, just having an emotional moment. It may sound at times like I am having all those experiences but I still want to avoid the journey cliché. I will add some clarity before journeying down that road.

There is a popular saying that every journey starts with a single step. This phrase can be superficially accepted to be true and, being positive, it has served as motivation for countless people in helping them get off their backsides, picking themselves up, pulling their fingers out, getting on with it, and stopping them making excuses. Are you counting? Don't count the clichés, make the clichés count is the old cliché. There you go; add that to the writers' self-help manual and put it on a motivational sign to hang on the toilet door in some journalists' office.

In a world where we all now seem to need to be more emotionally aware, the word "journey" has become over-used and, frankly, it is just a lazy way of avoiding making the effort to describe events that have had some significance, and explaining the significance and emotion of those events. In my case, I found myself being curious about my family surname and who my ancestors were, and this story tells of how I went from being curious to actually finding out. If I were to call it a journey then a certain phrase becomes very apt: "When does a journey end and when does it become a story?"

The journey has ended, the story has begun.

I have found more than I bargained for, although I don't know what I originally bargained for, so I will describe my feelings in this endeavour. The feeling of contentment surprised me more than I ever imagined and the sense of achievement came not only from *what* I found but more particularly *how* I found it.

In what follows I will try to describe my sense of contentment. I will qualify that and say *relative* contentment, because there is still something gnawing away at me making me think that there is still more to be discovered. In fact "contentment" doesn't really cover it; it is something deeper than that and I will explain later.

Story is a better description of what I am writing because "journey" doesn't do it justice; I need to tell the whole blow-by-blow account, including the digressions. Oh, and a minor point that the pedants will have identified – I did not start my journey with a single step; I started it on a bike and I wanted to avoid calling that journey a journey.

What I didn't realise before I started is that this was going to be something bigger and more time-consuming than a bike ride from London to Bath. In fact, it not only turned out to be immense but it became all-consuming and significantly more fulfilling than I could have imagined at outset.

Like others who have had quests, I thought my initial goal was clear. Unlike others, however, what I have found is so much more than the initial Holy Grail that I set out to seek. Despite apparently having a clear goal, I have found so much more than the family history that I had set out to find. It is not really what I set out to find; a simple name alone would be a result - but it would be boring, an anti-climax.

For those of you who have already jumped ahead and read the end of this book (**don't** do it, just **don't**) you will already know that I have yet to definitively find my grail, and like the theories on what the Holy Grail might be, I will provide the evidence and you can make up your own mind. Decide what it was that I set out to find and decide what it was that I did find.

I think I now have a clearer understanding – even if I have just confused you.

WHY DID I START?

The other day I saw a duck standing on the kerb waiting impatiently for a gap in the traffic. Then I saw a chicken approach the duck. The chicken stopped to offer advice. I heard the chicken say, "I wouldn't bother". The duck looked puzzled. The chicken turned, started to walk on, and looking over her shoulder said to the duck, "You will never hear the end of it…" That's me that is, the chicken; I don't know exactly why I initially crossed the road but those people who have asked me why will tell you that the end of the story is a long way off.

At some point you expect me to get on with recounting how I used the wisdom gained in my analogy about getting lost, right? Not exactly. In a way, getting lost has been more the solution than the problem. I have gone where there was previously no path and hopefully I have left an enduring, sign-posted trail for others to follow.

This story is about looking for something - but it is not that simple. The problem was that I didn't know what I was looking for, or where to find it, or even where to start looking for it. The good news is that I ultimately found it – "it" being what I didn't know I was looking for. Keep up or you'll get lost!

You are also possibly thinking that's a bit of a plot spoiler so early in the story but, to set expectations, this is not really about knowing the ending. It's about how I found "it" and learning what "it" is. More correctly, this is about learning what the "its" are. There's more than one "it" – which is that my auto grammar checker doesn't like there being more than one "it".

If the analogy is about getting lost on a journey, it may serve to first understand the reasons why I wanted to undertake this journey (that wasn't a journey). Let's start with this anecdote that may be familiar to those people with a name that is uncommon to someone else.

"Can I take your name, please, sir?"

"Colin Armorgie."

"Excuse me?"

"Colin. ARMORGIE." This time slower. LOUDER.

I can always hear the thought process at this point, and the conversation goes one of two ways, or even both ways, one after the other. It is frustrating because this is some sort of identification process, something that must be followed to allow something else to happen; usually something I am impatient to have happen.

Three, two, one… "That's an unusual name; where does it come from?"

In many cases, I don't think that the question is coming from anyone who really wants to know the answer or, if they do, they want a one word answer so that the social niceties can cease and they can get back to the more important things in their life, or whatever it is they were looking at on their mobile phone before I interrupted.

Of course, I wanted to know where the name comes from and I warn anyone against asking me the question now, particularly if you are in a corner at a party or stuck behind a reception desk. I will fully engage transmit-only mode and you will be caught in my tractor beam.

The origin of my unusual surname was one of my reasons for my quest. It was more correctly a quest at that point, rather than a journey; a quest being a trip to accomplish a specific task whereas a journey is where the trip is more important than the destination. Pedantic, I know, but I want to avoid overuse of the term journey - and I am failing.

The quest was to find out where the name Armorgie came from because, let's face it, it is an unusual surname. Like the man in the Johnny Cash song, A Boy Named Sue, I made me a vow to the moon and stars, to search the honky-tonks and bars to discover the man who gave me this name.

Is there a problem with having an unusual surname? Let's investigate. Armorgie begins with an A so I must have been first on the register in school, right? Not so: Abbot, Ancient, Anthony, Ayliffe, Armorgie. Fifth. Yeah, I know, it's just as well there wasn't a lad called Azziz in my class or he'd have been ahead of me as well. The reason for this anomaly in the class register, with Armorgie following Ayliffe, is unknown but it still rankles over 50 years later. These things matter to me, which, in its own way, is a reason for wanting to better understand my surname. I realise that I have a need for order in my life and for convention to be followed.

Part of the answer to "so what's the problem with having an unusual surname?" is that my name has shaped me as a person, and the reaction of others has become the trigger to release my inner cantankerous curmudgeon. Well, OK then, *one* of the triggers rather than **the** trigger. It doesn't take much.

Just how unusual is the name Armorgie? At the time I started investigating in the early 1980s, there was a sum total of 9 living people in the world who carried the name and one more that had been born an Armorgie and changed it on marriage. In fact, there had only been another 6 who had ever had the name and who were now deceased.

At the time of me starting writing in 2022, that total had risen from 9 to 42 who carried the name Armorgie, or who had married in, or who could claim the name. I have to admit that I am not sure if all those who have married in have actually taken the name, and I wouldn't blame them.

The significance of this statistic is that in the 151 years from the first, single official record of an Armorgie on the planet, the number has grown somewhat. Perhaps even more significant is that, out of that 42, there have only been 2 females born an Armorgie who have married out and taken another surname. That's not to imply that Armorgies are not the marrying kind, just that there have been a lot of males.

INTRODUCING SPERO

It's at this point I declare another level of mystery in the origin of the name Armorgie, perhaps a more compelling reason for my quest. It follows on naturally from me wanting to know where my name came from and is related to a possible 43rd person who had been an Armorgie who was equally likely not to have been an Armorgie. For this reason I had omitted this person from my reckoning when totalling all the people who had ever called themselves Armorgie. In fact, this person was arguably the very 1st Armorgie – his name was Spero Armorgie. I was looking for Spero.

This was no surprise to me, as family folklore spoke of Spero, the long lost relative who was something of an enigma. The name Spero was known, as this is the father's name recorded on my great grandfather's birth certificate. Apparently his recorded occupation was debated in family circles as being either a waiter or a writer as the handwriting on the certificate was unclear. This was the genealogical equivalent of a cold case; a whodunit, if you will. You can work out what the "it" was and what he "dun".

Spero or Spiro is a Greek nickname for Spyridon, who was a Greek saint. It is a very popular Greek name for boys and, based on that information alone, it had long been accepted family wisdom that we must therefore be descended from a Greek sailor who visited the UK. This was the *Gospel According To Frank*; Francis Bowden Armorgie is my dad and when I referred to "accepted wisdom", it was he who was the source of all the definitively unproven Armorgie family history – but he did tell a good story. To be fair, my family history research bears out most of what he told me to be true, and verbal history is one of the best sources of information in genealogical research.

I haven't polled the other Armorgies in this world about hearing the question, "where does the name Armorgie come from?" but I reckon they've all heard that same question many, many times. The same is probably true of anyone else with an unusual name.

Until I performed my research on the origins of the family name, my response to this question of where does the name come from was a shrug of the shoulders, sometimes trotting out the historic family wisdom mantra, "I think it's Greek…"

"You don't look Greek," is the response I have come to expect and I can imagine that's a relief for the population of Greece.

Amongst similarly illogical things they could say would be, "You don't look like a Colin."

Even before researching my family ancestry I had looked for clues in the make-up of the name Armorgie. I remember the revelation to me as a child in school, learning of the place, *Armorica*, which is the north-western part of ancient Gaul, corresponding to modern Brittany in France. That was the first of many "solved it!" moments in my life and that, like most of the others, got me into trouble.

"Paint a shield with a design to represent a coat of arms that describes your family," requested Mrs Davies.

For the benefit of the younger reader, a coat of arms is what you might now know as a "logo", like something on

AMERICA'S HOPE

the breast of a Ralph Lauren polo shirt but not necessarily a bloke on a horse. Oh, and let me introduce Mrs Davies; my primary school teacher and undeservedly serving a role as the butt of several jokes. She receives further bad school reports from me later in my story but she played her part in my interest in my family name and ancestry, and I disguise my gratitude.

In the coat of arms challenge, I know *now* that Mrs Davies wanted a selection of those heraldic devices that we'd been learning about in class, but I found a Breton flag. My thinking went a bit like a modern 'word cloud'. I say 'modern' as I was ahead of my time and word clouds hadn't been invented back then. Armorica, Brittany, Breton. In the school library was an encyclopaedia, an early, paper-based version of Wikipedia, if you will, and it showed the simple black and white horizontal stripes of the Breton flag.

"Solved it!" It took me about a minute to paint my shield with simple black and white horizontal stripes of the Breton flag. I ignored the other blobs, not for the first time in my life.

It appears that Mrs Davies didn't appreciate the honed skills of kids who had learned to work so efficiently that it facilitated an early finish. The time that was saved was not wasted either, and she should have been proud. Except she wasn't proud. I was able to slink off into the playground to work on my football skills. To her credit, however, at lunch times Mrs Davies did invite us really smart kids to join her for a bit of extra tuition, repeatedly writing the same line of "I must dedicate myself to what I am told to do blah, blah, blah…" It appears that efficiency and laziness are divided by a fine line.

It's just as well Pele didn't end up in her class.

Meanwhile, back at every social event, every hotel reception and every Indian railway ticket office that I ever visit, I am now able to use my new response to the "Armorgie: Where does that come from?" question.

"How long have you got?" is the carefully prepared, oven ready, off the shelf, ready to go, terse and crafted response. That usually shuts them up.

ONE OF THE FEW

I was a curious child. There are parts of me that are still both of those. See my wife for details.

I have long been curious about my surname. At school there were Smiths from different, unrelated families, but there were no other Armorgies, other than my brothers. I set out thinking that I wanted to find out more about my surname and where it came from, but that morphed into me finding a whole lot more than I ever imagined.

From this curiosity grew an interest, and from that interest grew a determination to find out, and from a determination grew a passion, and from a passion grew an obsession, and from an obsession grew this book. Through my research, I think at least my obsession has waned and has shrunk to being mere sustenance.

In terms of investigating a particular surname, having an unusual one presents opportunities and challenges. I know this, as I have spent years getting confused about what is an opportunity and what is a challenge; it kind of blurred after a while.

On the face of it, the uncommon surname should have made it easy for me to identify other Armorgies, including my forebears. That was true to a point and years of ancestry research has allowed me to feel the small, smug victory that hindsight has delivered. It turned out that before I started my ancestry research, I did actually know all those Armorgies who had ever lived on this planet and all those still living. More correctly, I should say that I knew of all those living… more on the phantom Armorgies later.

I say that I knew of those Armorgies who had ever lived on the planet as I had to put some boundaries to my research. The planet is planet Earth, to avoid potential confusion and mission creep. Knowing every member of the terrestrial Armorgie dynasty did not yet feel like "job done, let's go to the pub to celebrate", because it still didn't answer the question of where the name came from.

The answer to this is tied up in the fact that it turns out that Armorgie is not my real name, or rather shouldn't be my name if the rules of traditional British heredity had been followed. It also turns out that the name Armorgie has been linked to individuals who were not very good at obeying rules but had a talent for not always getting caught. I have some experience in this matter. The point is that sons and daughters should inherit the father's surname.

One initial possible reason that can be quickly dealt with is whether there have been surname spelling mistakes in the lineage? Not so - if it were that simple, I'd have been in the pub 40 years ago celebrating this discovery with drinks all round. I feel robbed that my surname quest has taken so long, as the beer was a lot cheaper back then. I have searched for connections to every known misspelling of the name Armorgie – and there have been many of those.

There have, however, been countless misspellings of the accepted form of the name Armorgie – just not in way that would give me a surname that I couldn't find. I have searched documented records for every common misspelling and it has presented no credible candidate for "Spero Armorgie". If I stop to think of the time I have invested in this search that has been condensed to this single paragraph, I would need therapy.

A-DAY: THE ARMORGIE GENESIS

Misspellings of the name Armorgie are common and are to blame for many things, such as cocking up the name change on my wife's passport after we married. I don't think it stopped the honeymoon. I certainly went on the honeymoon and, if I remember correctly, I think my wife came too. As I am neither a child of the 1970s nor a northern comedian, I ought to introduce by name to the story, Shelley, my wife – instead her being just "The Wife". She has the wisdom of Gentleman Farmer, as well as some of his other traits, and has been responsible for major breakthroughs in my family history research.

It turns out, in a very convoluted way, that the original name spelling may well have been misspelled, but only by a single letter. That sounds implausible - but you just need convincing. Come with me...

Who or what defines the correct spelling of a proper noun? In the case of my name, I have always taken the correct spelling to be what it says on my birth certificate, and to take this to its logical conclusion, it must be the way it was spelled on the first official document on which it was recorded. The emphasis on first is relevant.

The earliest record that exists of the name Armorgie was stored in the vault in my aunt's house. I say vault, even though it was cunningly disguised to look distinctly like an old biscuit tin. The document is the birth certificate of my great grandfather, Reginald Armorgie, who was born on 24 November 1871. I shall refer to this day as A-Day: The Armorgie Genesis.

There were obviously significant pieces of information on that birth certificate – not least of which is the date of the birth registration, which was not until Friday 29 December 1871, over a month after the birth. Why was it over a month later? Maybe the parents got fed up waiting for the Magi to arrive, I don't know.

The significance of date of birth registration is that it is the same date as the record of baptism of Reginald. So, on that day, which came first, the birth registration or the baptism? The reality is that the name was misspelled in the course of its first day of existence:

| Birth certificate: | ARMORGIE |
| Baptism record: | AMORGIE |

That's a good start. One of these is wrong, but which one? To one of them I can attribute a theory that has a further significance that comes into play when I find other information later in my search. Watch this space!

STORIES OF MISSPELLINGS

Other than the Armorgie / Amorgie paradox, there is another reason for saying that Armorgie is not my real name, and it is slightly more nuanced. This is based on experience and will be familiar to everyone with the surname Armorgie. In fact it will probably be familiar to everyone with a name that is uncommon.

Here is an example of an interaction that helps explain this, one that starts like, "What's your name, mate?"

"Colin Armorgie."

"How do you spell that?"

No, it's not déjà vu, this is an alternative conversation faced by all those with a name that others perceive as unusual. This is the alternative to the where-does-it-come-from path described earlier.

"A-R-M-O-R-G-I-E." I dictate, as I all too often watch them write it down as A-R-M-O-G-I-E. Yes, read that carefully again. It's like part of a Derren Brown[1] stage show featuring the disappearing letter trick. Is it really that difficult to write down every letter as I spell the name? The answer, I have come to realise, is yes, it sometimes really is

---

[1] English illusionist and mentalist who does spooky entertainment shows. He hails from the Croydon area of London, which you may later consider to be some sort of spooky coincidence; hold that thought.

that difficult. I don't know what is so hard about writing down all the right letters in the order they are dictated, but hey.

Actually, Derren, as you have wandered into my story, I've got a bone to pick with you. You are quoted as saying, "There are things in your life which you are in control of, and those you're not. You need to not care about those things which you're not in control of, and when you come to really understand that, you can go from being really upset about something to that lovely feeling of being a kid where everything is okay."

I am not in control of the name I was given, Derren, but I care about it, I care where it comes from, I care when it came into being, and I care what it might mean. I care a lot. That is justification for my upset, and the upset is justification for this book, and the reason that Mrs Davies gets repeatedly picked on. Sorry, miss – blame Derren.

Derren, I think I like one of your other quotes better: "We're terrible at realising what goes on in other people's heads because we are trapped inside our own." Oh, and if you are that smart, tell me how many fingers I'm holding up at the moment.

****

Sometimes I get the feeling when people ask me to spell the name Armorgie, that it is also a challenge to me. After I have spelled it, I get the feeling that they really want to ask the supplementary question, "Are you sure that's how you spell your name?"

It's a human trait to require conformity; we feel more comfortable if something is familiar. In my lifetime, more than one person has heard me say Armorgie yet has referred back to me as Mr Armitage, because that's a name with which they are familiar. Many people are much more comfortable when they can pigeon-hole you, so to have a

AMERICA'S HOPE

name that is unusual indicates non-conformity: You can't come in.

This is not dissimilar to the law that existed in France up to 1963 that prevented use of names, prénoms, that didn't preserve national integrity. Seriously – although following what I have already written, I realise that I am on shaky ground asking you to conform to my request to take me seriously. French parents were given the liberté to be more inventive – but not too inventive. After all, this is France that I am talking about. The French law currently states that a court can still ban names if they decide it is against the child's best interests. In a classic example, the prénom "Prince William" was banned by the courts, the reason being, according to the court, was that this could lead to a "lifetime of mockery". Perhaps worse than that for some holders of that name, it was lumped in with other inappropriate names like "Jihad", "Mini Cooper" and "Constipation" – The judge said of the latter, apparently, that it just wouldn't pass.

Part of this disbelief is down to something that doesn't come across in print, as it is to do with the pronunciation. For reasons of "that's-just-how-we-say-it", Armorgies pronounce the name as Are'mah-jee, with three syllables, with the same cadence, rhythm and soft G: as when saying "our budgie". Don't laugh, this is serious. So many other people naturally pronounce it with a hard G: Are'mah-ghee or Arr.More.Ghee. Of course, there is no right or wrong and there is no reason why we say Are'mah-jee, but it certainly pisses off certain younger members of the family when others say it differently.

I should say this has nothing to do with this story – I just wanted to get it off my chest. You know I said that I have got other things from writing this book? This rant is one of those cathartic experiences. Now, go on, say "Armorgie" to yourself a few times to get the hang of it – you may need to use it one day.

COLIN ARMORGIE

The annals of Armorgie history are littered with requests for spelling. My brother was once on holiday in Israel, back in the 1980s, and was asked his name by a hotel receptionist. He told them the name without spelling it and, to his astonishment, the receptionist transcribed it absolutely correctly, first time, without asking for the spelling. His partner, who incidentally liked the name Armorgie so much that she later married him just to acquire it, had the surname Smith. This flummoxed the receptionist: "And how is madam spelling that?"

Similarly, many years ago, I was in India trying to make a reservation for a train journey. I was fed up with spelling my name yet again, and thought I would short circuit the process (Mrs Davies, please take note; you'll like this) Now, bear in mind that my name was only to be used to label the seat on the train that I was eventually to be sitting in, no other reason. Yet again, I was deserving of what I got.

"What is your good name, sir?"

"London. Mr London."

"Brilliant," I thought! I was smugly confident with my inventiveness. Everyone knows London, no need to spell it, no quibble, and it won't get confused with the Indian names of my fellow passengers. Not so. There was a pause of the pen in the clerk's hand above the form. Without looking up, he said, "You cannot be Mr London because that is the name of the capital of England."

"No. No, I am. I am Mr London," my voice wavering, sounding less than convincing.

"No, sir, that is not possible."

"OK, OK. It's Mr Armorgie."

"And how do you spell your good name, sir?" If I say etcetera, etcetera, at this point, you can fill in the rest for yourself, although you are unlikely to feel the same frustration as I did. Now I know why there are bars on the ticket office windows at Indian railway stations.

AMERICA'S HOPE

Even in a modern world of simplified online ordering, the spectre of misspelling still haunts me. I ordered a piece of egoistical neon kitsch for my home lockdown bar; a sign that (should have) spelled the name "Armorgie" in illuminated pink neon. The order process involved me entering the text that I wanted to appear on the sign, so no chance of anything being lost in a verbal relay, right? All the manufacturer of the sign had to do was create it using the name that I gave them; just that one word.

I will skip the explanation of the initial outcome, it's obvious, and say that they got it right second time. Looking for the positives from this, they possibly drew upon my feedback and the experience for future quality assurance purposes; I don't know. The last that I heard was that the sign maker had found a new job opportunity working as a receptionist in an Israeli hotel. The bonus for me was that I was allowed to keep the misspelled original which I have grown to quite like and now use to demonstrate that five-pints-feeling to children, backing up my warning to them that a life of drinking alcohol will actually prevent progress in completion of tasks like building a home bar.

Sometimes, people unfamiliar with how to pronounce the name Armorgie will simply look to avoid having a go at saying it; clever. My brother, Roger, told me a story of when he used to work in the family hotel business with Dad, which must have been part of Dad feeling that Roger needed further tuition in those areas of customer service that he hadn't received in college. To give an idea of which decade Roger worked with Dad, the story Roger told me was of customers arriving for dinner in the restaurant, and amongst those, a couple arriving wearing shell suits. Very 1980s and very comfortable, I'm sure, but to my Dad they would have been in the category of fashion for nightwear or the beach. Not that he would have said it to anyone's face more than once.

COLIN ARMORGIE

That evening, Dad was playing the role of Mine Host in his normal style of Basil Fawlty and, to set the scene, Dad had previously never met Mr and Mrs Shell Suit.

"You must be Frank," stated Mr Shell Suit, offering a handshake as an introduction, and very cleverly avoiding having a go at saying Armorgie.

Dad was Old School, or more correctly, Ancient School, and to him such familiarity from a stranger was similar to a soldier of lower rank saying "bollocks" to the colonel of the regiment.

"I don't remember you being at my christening," responded Dad, "So to you it's Mr Armorgie, and let me spell that for you to prevent any further confusion..."

You are now adept at completing sentences that start that way, so I'll leave it up to you in the same way that Roger left recounting the rest of his story to me. I am sure Dad would have warmly shaken the hand of Mr Shell Suit, as that would have been the polite thing to do according to DeBrett's.

Possibly unrelated, but shortly after witnessing this encounter between the Shell Suits and Dad, Roger decided to have a change of career – of course, that was after he had received counselling to assist in unclenching his buttocks.

Please see the chapter on *Inheriting things that matter* to understand which of my father's qualities I may now exhibit with the passage of time.

SPERO BECOMES THE DESTINATION

Even before my experience of understanding what it means to be a recurring spelling mistake, there have been others before me that experienced those different spellings, the differences in pronunciation, the questions about the origins of the name, and the desire to understand our family history. Now it was my turn, so I grabbed the baton, stepped up to the plate and started to mix my metaphors like a bitter shandy. And similes.

Maybe it's the same thing but not only did I set out to find the origin of my family surname, I also wanted to **understand** my ancestry: Faces to names that I already knew, names to places where I knew the family had already been, why they were there, what they did for a living, their place in history. One relative, living, who shall remain nameless[2], only wanted to know where the family fortune is buried. My desire was pretty much to find out as much as I could, and that is still my aim but, in the shorter term, I had to have a more achievable goal. I settled for finding out who Spero Armorgie, my great great grandfather, really was. If shorter term is defined as being of 35 years duration, then

---

[2] A Daily Mail reader – there's your clue.

I achieved my goal on time. Oh, you are dying to ask; the family fortune *was* found and now enriches my soul.

So this was my quest, the allegorical journey-that-wasn't-a-journey on which I got lost by not starting in the right place, at the wrong time, seeking the wrong thing, for reasons that are hard for others to understand. What I did have, do have, is a determination to succeed – even if it is without Goals and Plans.

From my search for my Holy Grail I have taken other things, largely positive; things that I never expected to find or experience. *The Search for Spero* sounds like a film in the Star Trek franchise, and why not, as it has turned out to be a story worth telling. I think it is a great story as it has had the power to push me over the edge into writing it down here. In fact, it is more of a great-great story. Whether I am explaining myself in a great-great way is yours to judge. At the moment you are probably thinking, "Get on and tell the bloody story!"

It's my story and I'll tell it my time, in lots of words, just so you can feel that you are getting value for the investment of your time.

DIGRESSION

You will have observed that I have a tendency to digress. I could call it a tendency for me to be distracted but that would just be me deflecting the blame. In fact, this story has already acquired a feeling of one big digression, loosely meandering through the library that documents my life. All I can say is, please, stick with it as it does come together in the end and everything leading there is relevant.

This is all supposing that I can stay focused enough to discover the identity of my great great grandfather. You will also come to realise why it took me so bloody long to find him, if you haven't already.

"Stick to the facts, Armorgie!" I was so often told at school, so I learned to recount the facts but I also learned to retain the rich trove of trivia gained from my digressions in life, later to selectively dispense the trivia when required. Pub quizzes are an unexpected but liquidly rewarding outlet.

It is that great disability I have in being able to digress that is, at least in part, responsible for me having found out so much about my ancestry - and not only finding out so much about it but finding so much enjoyment and fascination in finding out about it. If I had stuck to finding the simple records of births, marriages and deaths, I could have opened my own records' office, but now, armed with the associated trivia, I can open minds.

I have learned why people lived where they lived, why they migrated, how they died, what they wore, what they ate, what they looked like, what they did as an occupation – and so much more. This is where world history has shaped family history and where family history has played its small part in shaping world history.

Whilst I am digressing, seeing my place in my family history is like George Bailey in *It's a Wonderful Life* being shown how the world would have been if he hadn't played his apparently small part. I find it very hard to comprehend that I would not be here if it hadn't have been for certain seemingly chance historic encounters and apparently unconnected events.

THE ARMORGIE SAGAS

"*History remembers only the celebrated, genealogy remembers them all.*" Laurence Overmire (American poet, author, actor, educator, genealogist, peace activist, civil rights, human rights, and animal rights advocate and environmentalist)

This was not the pithy sort of quote that I was seeking as a preface to this story but it usefully separates history and genealogy. My focus was initially on genealogy, studying the past and present members of my family and, if I went far enough back, you never know, I might even find that I was related to people who had a place in historical records. But then this would have been known and would have been handed down in family stories, surely? It turns out it wasn't known and therefore wasn't handed down.

What was handed down was nevertheless interesting and is a valuable source of genealogical information. The stories my parents, grandparents, aunts and uncles told of their relatives were like the Icelandic sagas, passed down verbally from them to me and my generation of the family, as the stories had been passed down to them. I came to realise in my genealogical research, however, that the stories were not all a reflection of reality. They *were* true, in the sense that no one had lied, but the stories had no basis in fact; they were just conjecture. I carry on that family tradition.

COLIN ARMORGIE

As part of my curiosity as a child, I remembering asking my father on more than one occasion, "Where do I come from?"

My father would speak of his great grandfather as if he were the mystery that I have found him to be. I don't recall my father every saying, "I don't know who Spero was". Dad was not given to saying "don't know". His answers would veer from vague guesses to humorous fabrication. This is where he recounted the Greek sailor myth as if it were gospel truth – because that is what his father had told him. On every re-telling, the details were changed slightly, but this could have been his way to make that difficult admission that he just didn't know – and we *should* know these things, right?

The last time I asked the "where do I come from question", he started his reply with, "Well, son, it's like this. When a mummy and daddy love each other very much…"

"Hold on, dad – I'm 23; I kind of get that bit."

"Kind of" was about right, but I lived in expectation.

The thing about Dad-Jokes is that, like genes, they are handed down from generation to generation and improve with repetition. Ask my kids. My Dad and I would joke about it, failing to accept our family failings regarding failing to know. Joking about it was an easy way to deal with our ignorance.

I used to be impressionable – hey, I was a kid – then I grew up and now I long for the days of innocence to erase my gathering cynicism. My father would keep my interest and, in doing so, would follow the example of Mark Twain in that he would never let the truth get in the way of a good story. It was a trope that he knew he employed and made no pretence about it. You see, much of Dad's working life had been as a salesman. Maybe my story is just me carrying on the family business.

This is why our family had nothing like the "family bible" that some families have to record their hatches,

AMERICA'S HOPE

matches and dispatches. If we had one, Dad might have had to put his hand on it and swear to tell the truth, so help him, God.

My mother, on the other hand, would pass on information in her family sagas as gospel truth. The stories she had heard from her parents were passed on exactly as she had heard them. As it turns out, those stories included the embellishments that were added by her parents, particularly her mother. Grandmother, Olga, was responsible for severely diluting the truth.

The sagas that my parents told were not in the cosy sense of us being huddled around the fire drinking bedtime cocoa on the long winter nights. They were usually recited on the seemingly interminable car journeys that punctuated my childhood. My three brothers and I, sitting line-abreast on the rear seat of my father's car, were bored as soon as the excitement had worn off from watching the family dog run down the road after us at the start of our journey. This could be nearly a mile on occasions when my father was trying to multi-task by driving whilst lighting his cigarette and reading the map whilst applying his usual pedal-to-the-metal getaway with us fighting the g-forces in the back.

There were countless times when we were at that place named Nearly-There-Yet, which was the place when the sagas would begin. I can't remember when I first heard any particular story because they were oft told and the story teller had a captive audience. That repetition was important because it meant that the stories stuck in my memory. Of course, Dad could have written them down like I am, but to a salesman that represented something that could be deemed to be a legal contract - something he carefully avoided.

Today, I validate my gradually failing memory with questions asked of my brothers, where we can usually piece together our memories to fairly reliably reconstruct Dad's unreliable stories. Those initial story tellings were delivered as family heirlooms to be shared like the family early-onset male pattern baldness. If you were less lucky, you inherited the ginger hair from Mum's Jackson side of the family. If only there had been more substance in the Jackson family wills other than a guaranteed full head of ginger hair.

It was from this starting point that my knowledge of family began. However, it was like the bag of numbered wooden balls used by the Football Association when making the draw for the FA Cup. I knew the names but they were as mixed up in my head as "number 1, Arsenal, will play number 29, Reginald Armorgie or Uncle Cecil."

It was for these reasons of the telling of verbal history that I was really unable to say when I actually started learning about my ancestry. It was always there. It still is. I like that.

INHERITING THINGS THAT MATTER

As my father told a good story, so did my mother in a different way. As I said, she would faithfully recount the patchwork of embellished truths she had been told, but she also had a filter to separate out those things that she really didn't want to tell.

As Mum grew older, we never realised that her mind was being cruelly and gradually robbed by dementia but, with hindsight, I now realise that this also had a wonderful, positive spin off.

The best moments in her later life were the simple things. She loved receiving telephone calls which were largely from family who couldn't be with her on a daily basis. Those conversations always started with me asking what she had been doing that day, and it was very obviously a struggle for her to remember.

"Not a lot," was the answer that came out every time, almost as a Pavlovian response. It was hard – hard for her to remember and hard for me to face up to the fact that the woman I had loved all my life like only a child can, the woman who had always had a sharp mind, with a wit and intelligence to match, was reduced to this.

If this was the apparent sad reality, how could there be a positive spin off? I failed to see this at the time but what she had was a life that was quite a rich mix of what I thought was mundane, but each little element had an importance to her. It was important to both of us to talk. In our conversations, she couldn't remember what she had eaten for breakfast, and I didn't want to know that if I am honest, but her recollections of her youth were crystal clear and she could talk lucidly in great detail. This I did want to hear.

More than the recollection of events in her past, the best bit for me was that her previous "embarrassment filter" had gone! She opened up to talking honestly about those things like she was on the Graham Norton Show; she spoke of things that she had never previously spoken of. And never would again, sadly. There were surprises and I was hungry to hear them all. Amongst the things she spoke of were the black sheep of the family, and I went on to investigate who they were, looking for clues about why they had been trimmed from polite family conversation. The exile of certain family member came down to reasons of money. Always.

Of course, I wanted to hear juicy gossip but Mum never mentioned any obscuring of family members for reasons of illegitimacy, which happened in many families of previous generations – that is both the illegitimacy and the obscuring. As it turns out, there was no obscuring because Mum and Dad apparently never knew about the illegitimacy – but then how would I know what they knew and wouldn't talk about?

WHY *WAS* I GOING TO BATH?

With the further benefit of hindsight, I can say that Mrs Davies, my primary school teacher, was in some way responsible for sparking an interest in my family ancestry. It was a slow burner to start with, then it took hold, and it wasn't until about 60 years later that I finally got it under control, but it still smoulders.

In the years after escaping from Mrs Davies, the firestarter, the twisted firestarter, there were diversions in my life that meant I didn't dedicate too much time and effort in the hunt for Spero. That didn't stop me *wanting* to know who he was and didn't stop the family discussion, usually about Greece, again and again. It spurred me to find the truth, like the words of another old Greek, Aristotle: "*Well begun is half done*".

My great grandfather, Reginald Armorgie, was baptised, and had his birth officially *registered* on 29 December 1871, the day when the first ever recorded reference to the name Armorgie was made. Reg was born in Bath, his birth was registered in Bath and he was baptised in Bath. I was equipped with the deductive skills to know where to start my search.

I'll give you a tandem ride back to the start of the story when I got lost while cycling to Bath from London. On that summer Saturday morning in 1986, I was not alone; I had two passengers, two metaphoric passengers who were my reasons for coming to Bath, two ghosts who needed exorcising. The first passenger was the ghost of Spero, and he was going to be exorcised by me finding out what he had to do with Bath. I thought then, rather naïvely, that a single day in Bath should be all I needed to crack it…

In a pub car park[3], I once found a sculpture made simply and exquisitely out of dry stones, like a dry stone wall. It is a perfect sphere of about 1.5 metres in diameter and there is a small plaque on it with an inscription that reads, "This dry stone sculpture is dedicated to anyone who's taken on a job that was bigger than they thought it would be." This digression is made to introduce my realisation that a single day in Bath was going to be insufficient to crack the aforementioned "it", just so you know that the end of story is not approaching.

When I told people that had I started searching for my unknown ancestor, one of them told me that it would take me at least a year for me to reach any sort of conclusion. I wish. I had no idea it would actually take so long; I wish I had possessed 20-20 vision back then, or at least the ability to see as far ahead as the year 2020.

Meanwhile back in the room…

Reg Armorgie's birthday was sufficiently close to Christmas for me to have self-appointed permission to make a reference to Charles Dickens' *Christmas Carol*. The Ghost of Christmas Past was this man, Spero Armorgie. I had to get to Bath to find him. Despite the story of getting lost, I did actually find my way to Bath, in a way that's pretty much a mirror of how I discovered the previously unknown parts of my ancestry – by determinedly heading west and looking for the clues on the way.

---

[3] Anything that starts with those words you know will be a digression

AMERICA'S HOPE

In that weekend in Bath I spent a largely fruitless day at the Central Library trying to find where and why Reg's mother, Louisa, and her "husband", Spero, had been in Bath in 1871. You have possibly guessed what I found or, more correctly, what I didn't find. I should have realised beforehand that Bath was an anomaly in my family history as all the known family origins on my father's side were from Liverpool, Ireland and Wales - other than the birth of my great grandfather, Reg. After he was born, the "family" moved to Liverpool. Why?

Was this running away from Bath for some unknown reason, for example to move for employment and opportunity in the boom town that was Liverpool in the 1870s? As I later discovered, it was the other way around; my great great grandmother, Louisa, had run away <u>to</u> Bath. Moreover, I discovered that she was not Louisa Armorgie at the time her son Reginald was born, she was Louisa Crossley, and had recently left her home in Leamington Spa, Warwickshire. She may have come via Liverpool and she certainly ended up in Liverpool a short time later.

During that weekend in Bath, I <u>did</u> find some information that I was later able to corroborate as relevant. When I say later, it was 34 years later. In my defence, I had to wait for the internet to become the phenomenon that it now is and for historical records from diverse sources to be digitised, indexed and made available online. I just had to be patient and wait for the internet to be invented.

I was patient, or side-tracked by life; the result was the same. Spero, Reg and Louisa were put back in the drawer labelled "Stuff To Do".

This minor breakthrough I found in Bath records at that time was in the Bath Directory for 1870-71 and gave the name and address of a Henry Crossley living and working as a carpenter in Bath. Was Henry any relation to Louisa? The address on Reg's birth certificate was not Henry

Crossley's, and neither address was on any current street map but they were both in the Walcot area of Bath.

As I later discovered, however, Henry Joseph Crossley was one of Louisa's older brothers who had moved to Bath where he had married in 1866. I found Henry Crossley's address on the 1871 census of England, taken on 2 April 1871, and Louisa was not listed on that census. Henry Crossley's address was, however, the address that was the one given as Louisa's residence on Reg's birth and baptism records on 29 December 1871. Oh, and no big surprise, there was no one called Spero who was resident at that address.

In fact, I have yet to find a record on the 1871 census for **anywhere** in the UK where Louisa was living. If I were able to find that, maybe I would find Spero was with her… or maybe she was out of the country?

The second ghost that needed exorcising in Bath was the Ghost of Christmas Present. Dickens used this to represent generosity and good will, which is what it was, I think. At that time I had an 8 year relationship that had just come to an end, and I was not really exuding generosity or good will. All my previous visits to Bath had been with this partner whose family were from Bath, although she was no longer there in person, she was in spirit. In that weekend in 1986 on my own in Bath, I had a chance to reflect as I self-medicated with Bath Ales' finest Gem of a pint, and the Ghost of Christmas Present was exorcised. I recovered something like a feeling of good will.

In this one trip to Bath, I had exorcised the spirit of one ex and drawn a blank on the spirit of a very distant ex. It was a balance of sorts; let's call it a spirit level. Come on! As I'm not using a ghost writer, I have to create my own puns.

As I left Bath on that occasion, there were some things obviously still missing: Who was Spero? Why had he been in Bath? Why was his son born in Bath?

I was left to puzzle on these things on my journey back to London. Over the years, I have found that some of my toughest conundrums could be resolved whilst on the saddle of my bike, but it didn't happen this time. Should I give up? The answer is on these pages, as you know.

It is no plot spoiler to say that on later trips to Bath and armed with other information, I managed to find what I couldn't in 1986.

SELF-HELP

Here is a notice I saw in the toilets in the office of a major UK bank where I worked.

UK Bathroom Etiquette

- Please sit on the toilet and do not stand on it
- Please flush the used toilet paper down the toilet and not the bin
- Please throw plastic cups in the bin and not down the toilet
- Please flush the toilet after use with your hand and not your foot
- Please use your hand to open the door and don't leave toilet roll on the door handle
- The sinks are for washing your hands only. No hand towels or toilet paper should be used as a plug

Look beyond the obvious

I use this sign as an example of how I learned to look at things in a different way, where I learned to look at the message in things that are not all they were intended to convey.

This sign in the bank's toilet forms part of other people's wisdom that I have collected in my life and I will take the liberty of sharing some of it here. The toilet notice has an obvious message, delivered in a blunt way but, given that this was at a major UK bank, it also made me think of something else - to be less trusting of others who would look after my money. Somewhere there was a manager who was less than confident in the toilet skills of his work colleagues but felt they had the necessary skills to look after the money of millions of people.

Don't make assumptions

This has taught me to not make ass-umptions, to not be an ass, and possibly how to properly use my ass but it has also taught me to look at things from the perspective of other people. I try to be aware that others are looking at me, and what I have written, in a way that may not be obvious to me. It is just an awareness with no ass-umption that I may not actually have got it right nor ever will.

Look once, look twice, look again

In the context of my search for Spero, I learned, often the hard way, that what I was seeking was not necessarily going to be apparent and is certainly not going to find me. Much of what I have found when researching family history has only been found when looking at something, like a document or image, a second or subsequent time. I get annoyed that I didn't see it at first viewing but take comfort that it's pretty low down on the scale.

Accept help. Gratefully

As annoyed as I get with myself for missing things, I get even more annoyed when Shelley sees it where I couldn't. I should say *grateful* not annoyed. Depending how organised I get, I may yet include an Acknowledgments Section in this book, but if it remains my uncollated, un-reviewed ramblings and digressions, then now is the time to express my thanks – and learn to actively seek the help of others. And accept it.

Advice

In a way, I have included this chapter to mention some things that I have learned when seeking Spero – more importantly, what I didn't *expect* to learn. If anyone can take this as advice in some way, then that is up to them, as giving advice is a tricky thing – although that has not always stopped me from doing it before.

At this point, talking of advice, Shelley is very much a contributor to my story, my biggest supporter in more ways than one, and always gives measured advice. In return, she tells me that I give sound advice, although usually she qualifies that to say it is more "sound" than it is advice.

Advice has to be appropriate and not only understood but the person being advised has to understand the value of that advice. It is a subtle difference but it should therefore be *taken* and not *given*. Please take what you want and leave the rest – or leave all of it.

In finding out about my ancestors I have found out a lot about myself; my emotions, my weaknesses and just my approach to dealing with life. I am far from qualified to give advice but I take the approach that in the land of the blind, the one-eyed man is king. In the context of a visit to the optician, I am also blessed with 20:20 hindsight, which is an advantage.

COLIN ARMORGIE

Be prepared

My investigation into my ancestry feels like at some point it turned into something else other than satisfying my curiosity; it had strong elements of spirituality and emotion. As I learned about the lives of my forebears, they became real people rather than names on certificates and faces in photographs. They will have celebrated births, birthdays, weddings, anniversaries, they will have laughed and loved, yet it is easy to overlook that they faced the challenges of wars, bereavement, hunger, ill health, failed relationships and the inhumanity of man to fellow man.

Gentleman Farmer advised me that I was starting from the wrong place, which I now know to be true in respect of my search for Spero, but he gave me no warning of the perils that might lay ahead in Bath. He should have warned me to be prepared for what I might find. Who knows what is hidden in our history that we don't know about? I didn't until I found it.

Keep an open mind

There is nothing inherently wrong with self-help books but problem is that I was not going to let them help me. How do I know that? Simple - I have never read one. Therein lays my advice to not make the same mistakes as me and close off an opportunity without first seeing what it's all about.

I thought I had a goal with my ancestry research and yet I was taken by surprise at what I ended up finding. The reward was as much in the things that I didn't expect to discover and learn, as it was in achieving my original goal - assuming that I actually knew my goal.

I am a member of that tribe who has never picked up a self-help book except when I was short of a drinks coaster, yet am setting myself as appearing qualified to give advice. I *know* that I should read more, possibly including subjects that I am blind to, although, in a way, I think I have read many books that have helped me. Many books, not just subject text books, contain knowledge from which I must have learned things without realising it – combine that with seat-of-the-pants learning from my mistakes, and I am the more knowledgeable for it. I maybe haven't fully made the transition from being more knowledgeable to being wiser.

The lesson you might take from this book is that self-help is more of a self-fulfilling prophecy. How so? I didn't feel like I did anything special to find out about my family history but I must have done, otherwise someone smarter than me would have found what I found but so much sooner.

The other school of thought is that what I found was just preordained, but if I think like that it will do my head in. Or possibly it already has.

Patience

I always get suspicious when I see someone start a sentence with, "to be honest" as it implies that everything else they have written might be of dubious origin. So, to be honest, it wasn't easy finding out anything related to family trees 40 years ago when I started looking. I had to actually get up, get out there, visit document archives, and talk to people. It was so difficult, in fact, that I took the easy option of waiting for 40 years for so many sources of information to be digitised and made available via the internet. I will give you more information about my procrastination when I can be bothered.

I really have to blame Tim Berners-Lee for not having pulled his finger out and invented the internet sooner.

COLIN ARMORGIE

Challenge

I have already said I should be less trusting, like I did with my Dad's ability to tell his version of the truth (so help me, God) so I have developed a cynical approach to evidence. Maybe cynical is too strong; analytical, challenging and seeking validation are probably more accurate. That is, unless a boss is paying me to reach a particular conclusion, which is my working career in a nutshell. I have to add the "not really" rider to that statement in case I burn my bridges.

To find the truth, I have learned to challenge the evidence and seek validation. I ask questions. I ask more questions. I keep asking questions.

I WAS UNPREPARED

"There are known knowns; there are things we know we know. We also know there are known unknowns; that is to say we know there are some things we do not know. But there are also unknown unknowns - the ones we don't know we don't know."

This famous quote by US Secretary of Defense, Donald Rumsfeld, is kind of apt to where I was when I started my family history research. I knew so much about my family history from what was related to me by my parents: The known knowns. I knew that there were things that I didn't know which is why I started my quest: The known unknowns. What I was unprepared for were the surprises, *the unknown unknowns.*

That paragraph just about made it past my grammar and spell checker but struggled to make it past my understanding. Move on – it gets easier.

The received wisdom from people I talked to when I started researching family history is, "Be prepared for what you might find". However, it is not unusual to be blindly self-convinced at outset that yours will turn out to be a boring family tree, and that there will be nothing to surprise or even shock you. If there were something lurking there to surprise you, you'd have heard about, right?

COLIN ARMORGIE

My family tree was just never going to be the first boring family tree in history - life doesn't work that way and I would be deluded to think it does. I went in to my ancestry research wearing my suit of Armor-gie. Nothing could touch me, apart from perhaps the pun police. I have been chastened. I can be moved by fictional drama when it is a well-told story, but with my own family tree I found, to my surprise, that it was real and it was personal, and it certainly was moving.

My family history tells me, at a simple level, who my family were but it also helps to explain why I am the way I am, and more crucially, the process of finding out has changed me in ways that I could not have expected.

There is no such thing as boring ancestors because every life, however short, tells a story. Two people came together, drawn by whatever forces, to create a new life. In the passing of that life there were many people who would mourn, who had been touched by that person's life, and those who continue to be touched by it.

The mystery of Spero was, and still is, all-consuming. I needed to know who he was; now I need to know more. I set out to just find out his identity and leave it at that. Things don't always turn out the way you intend.

Of course, I have found things in my family past of which I admit I wouldn't have chosen. I could have quickly passed it off as not having anything to do with me, along the lines of "you can't choose your family", but I found it to not be as easy as that. I have seen things that can't be unseen. There were things that I have found it hard to embrace, in equal measure to the things that gave me great satisfaction to know. Is it better to know or not know? There is only one correct answer.

By now you might have got a sniff of scandal in what I might have found. Hey, I've got to keep you interested. I have found who I think to be Spero and he is arguably no extraordinary man; he was an ordinary man who just had extraordinary circumstances that he had to deal with, and did so in an extraordinary way.

As it turned out, I was unprepared and I was surprised at what I found.

THE SINS OF OUR FATHERS

"You can't go back and change the beginning, but you can start where you are and change the ending." C. S. Lewis. Tell that to Gentleman Farmer.

The more observant will have already noted I never completed my Christmas Carol allegory; that's because it deserves its own chapter as its origins are a bit more contrived than that lightweight, Dickens, had to deal with. And it is something that was a burden, so very much a ghost that needed to be exorcised.

Remember, at the time I started investigating my ancestry in the early 1980s, there were only 9 living people, including me, with the name of Armorgie; I knew I was related to all of them, I knew all of their names but I had only ever met 5 of them – my Mum, Dad and 3 brothers. Taking me out of the maths, that left 3 Armorgies that I had <u>never</u> met. So here I was trying to find out all I could about my family history and yet there was a third of all *living* Armorgies I couldn't find! Actually, "couldn't" is incorrect – if I didn't seek, I was never going to find. If I was ever to complete the Armorgie jigsaw puzzle, it was going to look a little odd with missing pieces.

This was an example of "known unknowns" and I was blind to the irony of having "unknown" living relatives in a global family of just 9, whilst I was seeking dead ones. I refer you back to the start where I was lost, not only lost but starting from the wrong place and not knowing what I needed to find. Where was the guidance of Gentleman Farmer when I needed him? Oh, I remember, I pissed him off some time previously so that avenue was closed. My salvation this time came from other family members. I willingly show them more gratitude than I should have shown to Gentleman Farmer, possibly because if I don't they will hunt me down and beat the shit out of me. That's the good thing about closely knit families.

The 3 people called Armorgie, who were my known unknowns, were my uncle Reg, his wife, Pat, and their son, Phil. My father fell out with his brother, Reg, when I was a child. The detail and rationale is uncertain as it was no one's finest hour. It was a dispute over money but neither of them seemed to realise that if they cut themselves, it wasn't gold coins that came pouring out. It was complicated; I learned later that it was actually more complicated and uncomfortable than I really wanted to know, but I do now know and I can't un-know it.

The Ghost of Christmas Future wanted to show Ebenezer Scrooge that unless he didn't make changes in his life, there would be things that he would regret. As Scrooge had been blind to these, so was I. Here I was seeking to find my long-dead great great grandfather, Spero, and there were relatives closer to home that I had yet to find.

Lights in the Night Sky

I've already explained my inclination to mix my metaphors. I took you from deepest Africa to Middle Earth, and then to a Dickensian Victorian classic. Hold on, it's about to take off, I'm taking this to an astral plane…

My 14 year old daughter received a message from the ether. She was using some online social media and got a message from a girl who was surprised that they shared the same surname. She showed me and I was surprised that Armorgie was spelled correctly; it must be a genuine Armorgie! As if there's a fake. I had my signpost to a destination but realised that there was more than one destination I had to find.

As part of that experience, I learned that time doesn't stand still; my long-lost cousin, Phil, had grown up and had a family of his own. Talking about learning, I looked at it from Phil's perspective and learned, yet again, that maybe I was the long-lost one – but we covered that previously. I had more answers to find.

Close Encounter of the First Kind

Despite my daughter giving a lead from her online experience, it was actually old-fashioned print medium that ultimately led to reunification of the wider Armorgie family – and it doesn't get any more old-fashioned than The Daily Mail. I know that I shouldn't be so prejudiced through my stereotyping but they started it. My brother, Neil, saw a piece of frothy lifestyle journalism in The Daily Mail that was about a husband and wife doing a job and life swap: Phil "Amorgie" (do you sense a theme?) and his wife, Debbie. It mentioned the company for whom Phil worked so Neil gave him a call.

Close Encounter of the Second Kind

"Phil, there's a man on the phone who'd like to talk to you."
"Who is it?"
"Says his name's Neil Armorgie."
Silence.
"Phil? Phil?"

"Er, put him through – but make sure you record the call; it's probably a scam."

"Phil, what were you thinking of?" asked Neil. "The Daily Mail! The fucking Daily Mail! You're better than that, mate – you're an Armorgie!"

I'm not sure exactly how the conversation went, it possibly lost something in the Chinese whispers of telling a story, but I'll refer you back to the disclaimer at the start of this book, particularly the bit about there may be an inclusion of an odd element of fiction. As much as I now wish I'd been eavesdropping on that conversation, it was a seminal moment in Armorgie family history. No argument about money could stop it.

At this point, I have to emphasise that the bit in the disclaimer about lawyers should be referred to, as my statement here is just conjecture, although, come to that, there's a lot more conjecture in this story and it will take (the paid time of someone else's) lawyers to separate the two. Hopefully.

Similarly, with my blatant, liberal elite attitude I have probably burned my bridges when hoping for a decent book review from The Daily Mail literary editor. I will probably compound my crimes in the eyes of Viscount Rothermere, chairman of the Daily Mail and General Trust, as I present evidence that links my family heritage to immigrants and celebrities – assuming that having one's own Wikipedia page makes one a celebrity. Put that in the Saturday lifestyle supplement.

Close Encounter of the Third Kind

Neil and Phil arranged to meet in The Green Man pub in Berwick Street in London's Soho. There was a discussion about how one would recognise the other but, as it turned out, they needn't have bothered, as the apples that fell from two adjacent Armorgie trees were proven to be spookily

AMERICA'S HOPE

similar. Neil really didn't need to have worn that red carnation in his button hole; he spotted Phil at the bar reading his copy of that day's Daily Mail.

This encounter helped me in my search for Spero, as I knew I was looking for a handsome bloke, with good stature, wit and a special sense of humour[4]. OK, so it occasionally skips a generation – but I take solace that my kids are blessed. In a story where I draw lessons-in-life, physical appearance is one of those clues that shouldn't be overlooked.

Close Encounter of the Fourth Kind

The next encounter was when Phil and his family were invited to meet every one of the other 22 Armorgies who were descended from his uncle Frank and who shared the same surname. This was the 80th birthday party of my mother and the first physical and spiritual embrace of the wider, previously fractured family. Phil and Debbie's family had grown to four with the addition of two more Armorgie-lets, but had grown somewhat in terms of birthday card obligations.

For the mathematically minded, there were 26 Armorgies in that room but sadly two short of a full-house at that moment in history with the absence of Phil's mum and dad, my Uncle Reg and Auntie Pat. It was a missed opportunity as an ever expanding family makes it increasingly unlikely that all Armorgies on the planet will gather in the same place in my lifetime.

Back on Planet Earth

Of course, the strengthening of a family bond that comes from reunion doesn't change the past. Someone

---

[4] Phil, let me know if that's not exactly what you told me.

much wiser than me once suggested that we should work on the flaws that can be corrected and accept the ones we can't. The past happened and, like any telling of history, the point of view may change but the history remains as it was. What happens is that the context may become a little clearer. Pretending it didn't happen doesn't change it, doesn't hide any hurt, doesn't make any of us responsible for the sins of our fathers, and yet it is difficult to lose the feelings of guilt. Hold this thought as it becomes a recurring theme, a bit like my digressions.

I am no Simon Schama nor Alistair Cooke, but what I can do, in my own small way, is to tell *my* story in *my* way, and, as I face the final curtain, I'll say it clear, I'll state my case, without regrets - well, maybe a few, but then again, too few to mention. I will look for the positives, whatever they may be. The positive from this family reunion is that it was a lesson. No, I didn't go out and buy a prize turkey to share with my Cratchit Armorgie family, but I had those feelings of joy that typically come at Christmas.

Hope

The Armorgie family, recently reunited, could perhaps provide me with a clearer view of the reasons that I was seeking to know more about my family history. "Finding" the known unknown Armorgies made me realise what I was hoping to find in my ancestry research and realise what is important to me, really important. Spero, buddy, as puzzling as you are, it turns out that it wasn't just all about you, sorry.

SERENDIPITOUS BEGINNINGS

Given the big build up in the opening chapters, there will be anticipation to know where I actually did start my ancestry research. I'm trying to big-up the big reveal, so humour me. I feel that I must issue a warning here – the starting point turns out to be the most obvious and sensible starting point when researching one's ancestry, so feel free to skip this chapter.

Conventional stories start at the beginning and chronologically move forwards in time, through a big fat middle, until the end is reached. Less conventional stories start at the end and work backwards. Ancestry research should also start at the end and work backwards. Ta-da! That's where I started, with *me*, as I was the "end" and it was my family origins that I was investigating

Properly unconventional stories start, as do poorly planned bike rides, in the middle, then meander around in time and place, and struggle to get to the destination. Weird. I would never fall into that trap.

It turns out that the starting point *was* easy to find, although I admit now that Gentleman Farmer was right; bastard. I really should have known where I was and had some clearer idea why I was looking. I accepted his advice, rather begrudgingly, then throughout my search I was more open and grateful to accept help from others. I combined that with a fair helping of good fortune and some inspired reading of the clues from unlikely sources, and those have lead me to the happy place where I am now. Well, happy-ish.

With further benefit from my old friend hindsight, more crucial in the success of my search was the consideration of *when* I started, rather than *where*. The choice of when I started my search was not a conscious one, it was a consequence of certain almost chance alignments. No, that's not an astrological alignment, as far as I am aware, although I haven't checked because we Librans don't believe in all that nonsense.

I kind of started my ancestry research back in the 1980s but it didn't feel like research as I didn't find anything of significance back then. The truth is that I didn't find anything because I took the flawed approach of a young man; I wanted quick results without putting in any effort. Actually, I wanted the quick results <u>and</u> a summer trip to the wonderful city of Bath. I got half lucky; Bath was wonderful.

I still question whether there was an advantage or disadvantage to me having started researching in the 1980's. One school of thought says I have the advantage of being over 30 years better at it, the other says that I got frustrated, disheartened and cynical because of the lack of those things that are now enabling ancestry research. Someday it will make more sense to me as I will, yet again, be wise after the event, so I'll not let it trouble me now.

Like so many things that happen in life for no apparent reason, I previously hadn't realised the chance alignments that, on reflection, have affected me. This is why I am a convert to the belief of being wise after the event; the longer after the event, the wiser I become. Actually, I didn't realise this until just as I started typing this chapter, if truth be told. This was yet another case of my life being blessed with hindsight.

In March 2020 was the start of the UK government coronavirus lockdown, and that severely restricted much activity away from home. In the preceding year I stopped working for a living; I called it retirement but my employer probably called it a relief. I needed a project to occupy me in the long, long periods at home; something that involved me not annoying Shelley any more than I could help. With no work (ha!) and forced to stay at home, what should I do?

What should I do? Who's asking? No one warned me about the life conditioning that forces us to morally justify our own existence. In the world of work it happens without notice.

"What do you do for a living?"

"What did you do at work today?"

"What did you do at the weekend?"

Our lives have to be filled with doing stuff, our days have to be productive, we have to justify our existence, to be accountable, responsible, consulted and informed. Whilst in the world of work, my antidote of choice to this external scrutiny always used to be beer, but I can now manage to respond to any of those above questions, still fuelled with beer, but without guilt: "I do what the fuck I like", is the simple truth.

So what the fuck did I like? I had to choose.

"*Choose Life. Choose a job. Choose a career. Choose a family. Choose a fucking big television, choose washing machines, cars, compact disc players and electrical tin openers. Choose good health, low cholesterol, and dental insurance. Choose fixed interest mortgage repayments. Choose a starter home. Choose your friends. Choose leisurewear and matching luggage. Choose a three-piece suit on hire purchase in a range of fucking fabrics. Choose DIY and wondering who the fuck you are on Sunday morning. Choose sitting on that couch watching mind-numbing, spirit-crushing game shows, stuffing fucking junk food into your mouth. Choose rotting away at the end of it all, pissing your last in a miserable home, nothing more than an embarrassment to the selfish, fucked up brats you spawned to replace yourselves. Choose your future. Choose life... But why would I want to do a thing like that? I chose not to choose life. I chose somethin' else. And the reasons? There are no reasons. Who needs reasons when you've got heroin?"*

— Irvine Welsh, Trainspotting

This view could possibly be a widely held cynical preconception amongst the workers of the world that retirement is a life of rotting away doing fuck all. Who am I kidding? It's about heroin addiction (the quote, not retirement; well, not for me at least)! This serves to act as my allegory of the alternative to work that I chose; my work substitute was my ancestry research. Fear not, free spirit that I am, I am willing to break the code of silence and admit that I am largely weaned off it thanks to the help of Genealogists Anonymous – but please don't tempt me back to the dark side.

There was one more serendipitous final enabler which was part of my collection of chance alignments, and it was one to which I have previously alluded, one provided by courtesy of Tim Berners-Lee. The internet is one of those resources that has revolutionised ancestry research. No more does this research require physical trips to libraries, churches, military archives or Somerset House in London. This was the end of my previously mentioned, patient 40 year wait for the internet.

Just to show my awareness, I am fully aware that the internet has been invaluable but it is also the modern day equivalent of "the bloke down the pub" telling you something - or my dad telling me something; same thing, really. I treat with caution what I have found on the internet and, by extension, you should treat with similar caution what I have written - maybe with even *more* caution.

None of these "enablers" would really work without a fuel. There was something that had always been with me but something that ramped up its influence exponentially as I started to get results. As I previously mentioned I had a *passion* for wanting to find out, and it grew to be more than that; it became a need, an obsession to find out.

THE OPENING CEREMONY

I had the opportunity, I had the motive, so I was ready to set off to mix my metaphors again and start exploring, even if it was in reverse gear. No wonder I had previously got lost.

It may come as a blessed relief to hear that I am omitting about 90% of what I found. Everything I found was interesting to me, and remains so, because everyone's life story has its own fascination to those who are interested. If you've got this far reading mine, you've either been paid to read it, you are a lawyer, or you are genuinely invested in it.

A family history is more than just births, marriages, and deaths. Everyone's life has a story to tell, but the mystery in my family tree was Spero Armorgie and, with that, the answer to the mystery of where my name came from. If you want a measure of just how unusual I found my Armorgie ancestry to be, I am actually skipping over the trivia which includes me omitting a description of my discovery of close family relationships to **living** sports stars. I have tongue-tying fan-boy enthusiasm for anyone who has achieved something in sport at a high level, and have found previously unknown family relationships to both an Olympic gold medallist and also to a captain of the men's

Welsh rugby union team. The fact that I am omitting their details here is an indication of my focus on my quest being reported here.

To further underline what really amazed me, I am also actually skipping over three generations of Armorgies in one paragraph. These generations are my generation, my father's generation and my grandfather's generation. My life has been... well, it's a long meandering tale of getting lost so I'll skip over it. In my father's generation, there were just two Armorgie males, and in his father's generation there was just one who survived into adulthood, my grandfather. Nature, it seems, had a way of playing its hand in keeping the name alive – my father and his brother produced five sons. To say that the rest is history is somewhat unnecessary in the context of a story about history; family history.

In those generations there was a certain economy in naming male Armorgie descendants. My father was Francis Armorgie and his brother was Reginald Armorgie. Their father was Francis Reginald Armorgie – and, as previously mentioned, his father, my great grandfather was Reginald Armorgie. What happened to the name Spero, the name of my putative great great grandfather? And where did the name Reginald come from in a family, like so many, where forenames are inherited like receding hairlines? These names were analysed and over-analysed by me as potential clues as I didn't want to overlook the obvious. You could call it an anal (-ytic) attention to detail. I know, I shouldn't have to signpost puns at this stage but I'm taking no chances.

It was in the course of my research into the life and times of Reginald, son of Spero, that I realised that there was a lot to discover - and it wasn't as straightforward as born, married, died; far from it. Let's start with the birth and inconsistent records that surround it. The earliest documented records of Reg's life were his birth certificate and baptism record, both in the city of Bath in 1871. His given surname was Armorgie or Amorgie depending on the source document; he was nominally the son of Louisa Armorgie, who was actually Louisa Crossley, and Spero Armorgie, who was… well, that's what we are going to find out. Louisa's given address was in Bath.

I have found out that not only was Louisa not married at that point in her life, but that Spero Armorgie did not actually exist; not a sniff of a record, misspelled or otherwise. Someone must have accompanied her to the baptism at the church, posing as her husband, but his real identity was the mystery that sparked my investigation and has consumed me - and consumed so much of my time, willingly given.

More than this doubt about the parents' names, when Reg was one year old in January 1873 his mother, Louisa, married William Long and Reg became known as Reginald Long. From all the documents I could find, Reg was known as Reginald Long until he married in 1893, at the age of 21, when he chose to revert to being called Reginald Armorgie – temporarily, as it turns out. There is no documentary evidence that indicates William Long might have been Reg's biological father and, having taken a DNA test, I have no genetic evidence that would support that either.

It is therefore likely that Reg not only didn't know his given name that was on his birth certificate but also probably didn't know that his father was called Spero. When he did find out, there must have been an interesting, possibly difficult conversation with his mother. Did his mother ever tell him who "Spero" *really* was? I wish I knew.

THE MAKING OF A SCOUSER

Louisa Crossley was born in Leamington Spa in 1845 and gave birth to Reginald Armorgie on 24 November 1871, then she registered the birth and had him baptised on 29 December 1871. By July 1872, she was back in Leamington Spa, or at least Baby Reg was because he has a vaccination record showing this. Then, in January 1873, just over a year after Reg was born in Bath, Louisa Crossley married William Long... in Liverpool, England. Why Liverpool? Louisa is recorded as a spinster and William a bachelor; the implication of this is that Louisa was not married to anyone when Reg was born. Was William the man who was posing as Spero Armorgie at the church in Bath on the day that Baby Reg was baptised? If it was, why didn't he put his name as the father?

William Long was about the same age as Louisa and was born in Somerset, about 30 miles south of Bath. Louisa and William gave the same Liverpool residential address on their marriage certificate. William and Louisa's occupations were both given as "servant". Unremarkable... except that this one document contained the information that held the key to me finding my metaphorical way to Bath. This was the documentary embodiment of my old friend, Gentleman Farmer, who, incidentally, was right about choosing the right place to start a journey; bastard (not for the first time). Er, actually, that term of abuse is perhaps not the one I should be using in the context of what I described in the previous chapter. Moving on…

When Louisa moved to Liverpool and got married, where was Baby Reg? Did he stay with Louisa's family in Leamington Spa or move to Liverpool with his mother? The first record that I found of him in Liverpool was a report of 24 November 1894 in the Liverpool Mercury newspaper that read:

A CASE OF SUSPICION - Reginald Armorgie (23) and Henry Charles (26) were charged with being unlawfully in possession of a quantity of lead and tools, and were remanded for seven days.

This was not the way that I expected to progress my search but this appears to be the making of a scouser, the start of a scouse family dynasty and why I have the red blood of a Liverpool Football Club supporter flowing through my softy southern veins. It was also, by the by, slightly surreal that this court appearance was reported on Reg's 23rd birthday. Fortunately, if there is any good fortune in this, there was no record of Reg being convicted – at least not on that charge.

That was the first record that I found, and when I later mentioned it to my cousin, Peter, son of my father's older sister, he knew about this from family folklore. He also asked what name Reg was using when he was caught. What? Did Peter also know that Reg had been living as Reg Long? Not only that but Peter was aware that Reg had also been known as Jack Bowden. Someone had changed the signposts on the back roads to Bath. Again, this was a key piece of information that opened the door to me finding out more about my great grandfather. You may notice that Bowden was my father's middle name. You may be confused. One of my Dad's grandchildren has also

AMERICA'S HOPE

inherited Bowden as a middle name. Explanations will be forthcoming, fear not.

That first record was not the first *chronological* record that documents Reg's life in Liverpool. My cousin, Peter, had inherited the family trove from his mother and amongst this was a *copy* of Reg's birth certificate that had been prepared on 21 August 1879 to satisfy the provisions relating to proof of age under The Elementary Education Act 1876. Reg would have been 7 years old and, on this same document, was recorded living at that time with his mother, Louisa Long. They were living at 85 Vine Street, Liverpool – the same address where they were living 2 years later in 1881 on the census of England and Wales. In that census, Louisa is recorded as living with her husband, William Long, plus Reginald Long, aged 9, and his 3 younger sisters.

Reg's changes of name throughout his life were surprising if not confusing, and making research of his life quite difficult. When posing as Jack Bowden he also used the more formal, yet deliberately obfuscating name of *John* Bowden. It later caught up with him, causing an administrative headache.

Reg may possibly have gone by other names but I have yet to find any of those, although I think there's another surname he *should* have been given by traditional paternal inheritance. In his time as Reginald Long, I found evidence of his next brush with authority. He appears to have left Liverpool, possibly out of need, I don't know, as on 4 May 1884, aged 13, Reg is mentioned as being admitted as an inmate to Her Majesty's Prison in Wakefield, West Yorkshire, England. I feel the need to add 'England' in the location description because later in life Reg furthers his career by grabbing various international opportunities.

Reg was convicted of stealing 12 shillings and 6 pence (equivalent to about £83 in 2020). The penalty today for such a crime in England might be a fine, more harshly a suspended custodial sentence, perhaps, but under the

Victorian legal system Reg got 14 days hard labour followed by 5 years detention in a 'reformatory'. At age 13, Reg was recorded as being a 4'4" tall errand boy whose place of birth was given as Antwerp. Antwerp? I don't know from where he got that notion of his birth place but it will later play its part in my evolving conspiracy theory. File it away in your memory for later reference.

Reg served every day of those 5 years in detention, as there was no probation, being discharged at the age of 18 on 16 May 1890. This was the nature of the penal system in England at that time. The first Reformatory Schools were set up in 1854 and young people were sent there for long periods, as they were designed to break the child away from the "bad influences" of home and environment. Reports that I have read about the treatment of young people in these institutions suggests that it was far from a farm-stay holiday or dude ranch. Transportation to Australia had ceased in 1868 as a sentence to crimes in England but, as it was, he spent 5 years at Calder Farm Reformatory School near Huddersfield. That didn't stop him later making his own way to Australia.

I know the Wakefield prison record was that specifically for my great grandfather because it shows that he was from Liverpool and that he had visits from his parents, Louisa and William Long. During his stay there, he was baptised a second time - but not his last! Again, this hints at Reg having little details of his early life. It makes me think that, if baptism represents the forgiveness and cleansing from sin, then repeated baptisms represent how Reg was attempting to keep on top of things.

"Be prepared for what you might find", you will recall, is the advice that is given to those researching their family history. I had to accept that Reg had a criminal record. It was the same revelation when I found that my cousin, Phil Armorgie, was the only other Armorgie with a record -

although Phil's record was a product of him being a musician.

When Reg was discharged from Reformatory School, his probation record shows him briefly living back with his mother in Liverpool, but in early 1891 he had moved out, was living locally and was "out of employment". There wouldn't have been a lot of room for an unemployed 18 year old in that house as his parents had another 5 children by now, and Louisa was 8 months pregnant, and there were 4 lodgers living at the address as well.

A month later, on the census in 1891, Reg was still lodging at the same address which was next door to his probation officer, Mr Menzies, who was a boot repairer by trade. This appears to have had significance in Reg's life and Mr Menzies may well have had more of an influence on Reg than just being his probation officer. A year later Reg was recorded as living again at his mother's house, and his probation record says that he "had recently returned from Scotland where he had been working". Maybe he had been staying with relatives of Mr Menzies, who was from Glasgow? Maybe this was part of Reg learning to be a shoe maker? I say this because, two months later, Reg is recorded as being a shoemaker in business for himself, with his own shop in Liverpool.

Having finally got some stability in a previously turbulent life, in March 1893 Reg gets married in Liverpool to Mary Elizabeth Bowden. Ah, there's the Bowden connection that you were waiting for! Reg's occupation is shown as shoemaker but, significantly, ta-da, Reg is now calling himself Reginald *Armorgie*, not Reginald Long. Reg has obviously seen his birth certificate as his father is recorded as "Spero Armorgie (deceased)". To paraphrase Mark Twain in his telegram to America from England, "The reports of Spero's death are perhaps greatly exaggerated". I will make a later case for Spero being something other than deceased on this date in March 1893.

COLIN ARMORGIE

Nine months later the next generation of Armorgie is born. Reg and his wife had a daughter, Alicia Ann, in December 1893. Alicia died in the post-WWI Spanish influenza epidemic in 1918. She died without children of her own. My grandfather, Reginald Francis, was born in 1895 and his brother, William, was born in 1899. William lived only 6 months. Throughout this marriage and raising a family, Reg carried on his business as a shoemaker - with a possible side-line in recycling lead from the roofs of Liverpool buildings.

I am not sure what happened in Reg's life but the next record I found after Reg's court appearance was as a fireman on the ship SS Lynton when it docked on 26 January 1900 at Albany, Western Australia, arriving from Melbourne. That was a long way from making shoes in Liverpool, and a long way from his wife and 2 children. Reg, Gentleman Farmer would have advised that if you wanted to get on the straight and narrow, you perhaps shouldn't have started from the other side of the world.

Yes, it begs the question of why Reg went to sea. I am able to speculate on other, less obvious, aspects of Armorgie family history and can only guess that in Reg's case he was avoiding justice; not for the first time. Or the last.

Where else did Reg end up? I have one other equally bizarre documented record showing Reg on the Norwegian census of 3 Dec 1900 in Kristiania, the port for Oslo, Norway. His ship was given as the *Fido* from Hull, England. Just weird. Had my heritage been associated with the surname Smith or Jones, I would never have found records like these. Having the name Armorgie has its advantages and disadvantages, although I am left wondering where else Reg ended up under some other assumed name.

Almost as if nothing unusual had happened in the preceding years, Reg is recorded on the 1901 census of England and Wales, living with his wife and two young children in Everton, a suburb of the city of Liverpool. I had never questioned it before but this also raises the equally weird, unsolved mystery of how the Armorgie family are Reds, not Toffees[5]. I suspect Reg's decision to relocate may have mirrored Everton's decision to relocate. Everton were one of the first members of the English Football League, the club founded in 1878 and who played at Anfield stadium. For those more perplexed about football than about the Armorgie origins, Anfield stadium is the home of Liverpool FC. Everton FC were evicted from Anfield in 1892, and the stadium was left empty with no team to play in it. The stadium owner decided to form his own team and, on 3 June 1892, Liverpool Football Club was born. The rest is the stuff of legend, a bit like the Armorgie family. I digress again...

Roscommon Street in Everton, where Reg and his family lived, and where he had his shoemaking business, was in the heart of that part of the city where Irish immigrants settled in the 19th century. Mary Elizabeth ("Lillian") Bowden was born in Liverpool of Irish parents and this probably explained why I found Reg acting as a confirmation sponsor at St Joseph's Roman Catholic Church in 1908. Having twice been baptised into the Church of England Reg must have converted to Roman Catholicism at some time for which I can't find a record, and been baptised again! Reg and Lillian did not marry in church so I don't think his change of religion was necessarily connected to his marriage. Reg was possibly the first fully committed Liverpudlian Catholic atheist.

If you are wondering why I choose to mention religion, it is because of its importance in Liverpool history, as well as it being analogous with another theme of divided communities that I will write about in later chapters. During

---

[5] Reds are supporters of Liverpool Football Club and Toffees are supporters of Everton Football Club.

Reg's lifetime there was a very strong sectarian ('orange' versus 'green') divide in Liverpool and this very much soured relations between Liverpool's residents. Sectarianism divided the city's politics, affected employment options, life opportunities, sparked street clashes and determined where people felt they could safely live. Liverpool life continued to be influenced by religion until the mid-1970s.

In fact, in 1909, a procession from that same St Joseph's Roman Catholic Church, where Reg acted as confirmation sponsor, was met with organised protest from Orangemen who were subject to apparent unnecessary force from the police and the whole thing triggered 5 days of violence in the city. A government inquiry labelled Liverpool as 'the Belfast of England'. I think Belfast asked for a second, independent opinion.

Reg's acceptance of the Roman Catholic faith, or the Roman Catholic Church accepting Reg, may have played a part in the next turbulent phase of his life, but I suspect it was also triggered by a need to disappear, yet again. Armed with the knowledge that I learned about Reg assuming the identity of Jack/John Bowden, I managed to track down and acquire a copy of his military service record in World War I. The immediate surprise was that he joined up in 1914 at the age of 43.

Volunteering to fight for a cause is not unusual but in Reg's case it is less usual because of the age that he joined up. War is normally declared by old men and fought by young men. More unusual than Reg's age are a whole host of other things that, almost certainly unintentionally, could read like some sort of attempt at redemptive behaviour for apparently having lived a life that was less than exemplary.

Having previously been known to be living and working in Liverpool, Reg enlisted on 31 August 1914, just over a month after the declaration of war, but he enlisted in Naas, County Kildare, Ireland. He joined the Royal Dublin Fusiliers under his assumed name of John Bowden, and I don't think his choice of joining an Irish regiment was necessarily anything to do with wanting to join and serve with men from his community in Liverpool, because Liverpool had its own territorial unit, the Liverpool Irish.

In April 1915 the Dublin Fusiliers were landed at Gallipoli. I don't know if Reg was amongst the soldiers who were landed on the beaches but I do know that of the 1,012 Dubliners who landed, there were just 11 who survived the whole Gallipoli campaign unscathed. If Reg had signed up as way to avoid problems that he may have faced Liverpool, he had got himself in far too deep now to consider Plan C in his book of lifestyle choices.

Reg's son, my grandfather, also enlisted to serve in WWI but this was over a year later than his father. Grampy more conventionally enlisted in the Royal Engineers Postal Service because he was working in Liverpool post office, as he did all his working life. Grampy was invalided out after about 6 months serving in northern France, and I don't think it was because of a paper cut.

Reg (senior) not only survived his service in the Gallipoli campaign but he served in the military until 3 months *after* the end of the war. Part of the reason for his survival was that his role was as the regimental boot maker; using the skills he bought from Civvy Street rather than just being cannon fodder. Some might say he was skilled at dodging the bullet. He also served time behind the front line in Italy where the wounded were being taken. Again, using his skills with working with leather, he was making walking aids and prosthetic limbs for amputees and wounded soldiers. At some point, understandable given what he was doing, Reg transferred from the Royal Dublin Fusiliers to the Royal Army Medical Corps (RAMC).

Great grandfather Reg may have been a bit of a scally, to use a Liverpudlian description, but his military service, and that of Grampy, were just more brilliant examples of where Armorgie family history overlapped with other significant events in world history. In fact, when it came to national service, my Dad also survived playing his part in Adolf Hitler's downfall. I think Dad's survival was likely related to that military saying, "there's a bullet out there with your name on it" because, as we know, no one can spell Armorgie, so Dad was safe.

After his death, his widow Elizabeth Armorgie, is recorded as being in receipt of a widow's pension for her spouse, *John* Armorgie. Are you keeping up? Reg's name was changed again but, notable and worthy of celebration, the surname was spelled correctly even if his forename was wrong. This was the administrative headache that I earlier referred to, as I found a whole sheaf of documentation that Elizabeth had to gather to prove her relationship to a bloke called Reginald Armorgie who never technically fought for his country. Proof of the marriage was easy, but explaining why Reg Long got married as Reginald Armorgie, yet enlisted as John Bowden, was more problematic.

In August 1918, Reg was back in Liverpool in a military hospital suffering with paratyphoid, followed by a period of home leave. The home leave, I think, was also associated with the death of his daughter Alicia on 13 October 1918. The war ended on 11 November 1918 and then, on 19 February 1919, Reg was discharged from the military as physically unfit with bronchitis and arthritis. The notes of the discharging Medical Officer stated that Reg would have recovered in 3 months. He did – sort of.

Reg's recovery was a false dawn as it turned out; he died on 9 May 1920, and it seems somewhat unjust that he survived the whole of WWI yet died of pneumonia 15 months after having been discharged from military service in a campaign where the odds of survival were less than good. There is no formal connection but Reg's pneumonia was quite possibly due to the effects of the Spanish Flu that took the lives of so many in that period after the end of the war, including his daughter, Alicia. Like so many of us now after the Covid-19 pandemic, I'm an expert in how contagious viral infections do their dirty work and how the cause of death is recorded without naming the guilty virus.

EPIPHANY

Reg was 47 years old when he died; I will qualify that by saying that he was *only* 47. When I found this out it felt to me like his life was taken too early, but my judgement was made on my idea of life expectancy today, just about 100 years later. In 1920, life expectancy for males was 56 yet, even so, it still does feel too early. He may only have lived for 47 years but he packed more things of note into his life than many people today who live much longer.

The previous chapter was disproportionately long compared to Reg's short life. This is because Reg lived a full life; full of things that could have made up the fascinating portions of the lives of more than one man. There would undoubtedly have been many more things of note in Reg's life that we know nothing of. To put it into context when I stop and think about it, I feel like I now know more about my great grandfather's life and times than I do about my own father's.

The informant of Reg's death was his wife, Elizabeth, and Reg's occupation was recorded on his death certificate as Master Shoemaker. This one document of his life, more than any other, still moves me emotionally in a way that surprises me. After all the things he suffered in a turbulent, wayward life, perhaps not all in his control or of his making, he had achieved something that I think is worthy of merit, and he had stopped running away, and he was still connected to his family.

Winding the clock forwards to the year 2020, many years after my initial bicycle pilgrimage to Bath, I happened to be in Bath yet again. Yes, it's been a less than straightforward journey, as I have already mentioned. It feels like a bit of a theme but it was purely coincidental that, this time again, I arrived by bike. I cycled with Shelley the full 16 miles from our home into the glorious city of Bath.

For reasons totally unconnected with my family origins in Bath, I now live conveniently close to Bath – in fact, there was a period of about a year when I worked in Bath and cycled there every day. It was the Best Commute Ever and the job never succeeded in spoiling my every day good mood. I am not discounting there being maybe some other force of fate at play that has placed me so close to Bath. Some people say that everything happens for a reason, preparing us for something that is yet to come.

Amongst other little facts that have no apparent reason, it is a meteorological fact that the sun always shines in Bath. On that early summer's day in 2020, once more, Bath's honey-coloured stone buildings were glowing in the hot sun and welcoming me to the place that has acquired special significance. This time I arrived with a strange feeling that is hard to describe, not the bitterness of a broken relationship this time, but strange in a good way. I couldn't initially put my finger on it.

This was 21 years after the death of my father and almost exactly 100 years since the death of my great grandfather, who had sometimes been known as Reginald Armorgie since he was named in that city. I was now armed with the knowledge of the Armorgie Genesis that I had gained from my early ancestry research in my retirement, and I was going to use it in my role as Family History Tourist. It felt like the city belonged to me for that day and it was spookily, preternaturally quiet, possibly in reverence to the intent of my visit.

Every summer in Bath, from Regency times, I imagine that there have been crowds of visitors - *except*, that is, for this very short period in 2020 during the Covid-19 pandemic lockdown. We walked north out of the city centre, under the shade of the plane trees, and then across the bridge that connects the city centre with London Road, crossing the River Avon. The roads were busy, they always are, and people seemed to know where they were going and, quite likely, knew where they had come from. The pavements, however, were almost free of pedestrians. If we ever met anyone else out walking, they gave us a wide berth. I don't blame them; I was infected with the spirit of optimism.

We crossed to the other side of London Road where the neighbourhoods of Walcot, Camden and Larkhall rise from the river – and rise they certainly do. That side of Bath has some roads that are so steep that they have steps cut into them, handily, so people can sit, admire the view and recover for the attempt on the summit. This I know.

I had done my homework and knew from Google Street View where I was going, which was a challenge as some of the roads had changed their names from the 1870s. I found the house where Reg was born, which is still there but surprisingly hasn't yet acquired its Blue Plaque. More correctly, this being Bath, notable residents are commemorated with more ornate, *bronze* heritage plaques. The absence of a plaque I will accept as being better than appearing on a poster that asks, "Have you seen this man?"

Photographs were taken, naturally, but they felt almost superfluous to my actually being there. The images were detached from my emotion and sense of history of what I was looking at. We walked down the hill from the Nativity Grotto towards the church of St Saviours where Reg had been baptised on 29 December 1871. The church is located in a residential urban area but on that day as we strolled around the churchyard, I was swallowed in the moment and oblivious to the rest of the world. The birds in the trees sang the theme tune to this scene in the film of the Armorgie Story.

These feelings don't leave you.

This was it. This is why I had a strange feeling that day. Everything became clear. Standing silently on the steps of the church, I was there, in that exact same place where Louisa and Spero had stood with baby Reg so long ago, so not so very long ago. I was there and, try as you might, you couldn't have prised me out of the DeLorean.

I wanted to go inside the church but the door was locked, it being during lockdown and this not being the door to 10 Downing Street. As I tried the door handle, there was a man inside the church, maybe the verger or the vicar, who gestured to me in a way that reinforced my faith in organised religion. Maybe he still harboured concerns about the lead on his church roof.

On that same day back in 1871, Reg's birth certificate makes it clear that the birth was registered by Louisa, *not* by Spero and not by Louisa and Spero as a couple. I don't know if it were usual back then for just the mother to register a birth but it would have been a different expectation with a baptism. Reg's baptism on the same day would likely have involved someone in the leading man role playing the part of Spero in person[6]. File this thought away for later, as it gains significance when I add conjecture to fact. Yes, conjecture, as I have to join the dots to link all the facts to construct a theory. You will be the jury on how well it hangs together.

For the moment, stop to consider that with this apparently small detail of names on registration documents,

---

[6] Let me translate for the youngsters: "...would likely have involved someone else *rocking up* as Spero."

or absence of a name, something didn't add up. Perversely, if it *had* made sense in simple terms of married-parents-having-a-baby, then I possibly wouldn't have directed my research where I did. Who knows? This is just one of several conundrums and unanswered questions that drove me on as the story started to write itself. I will provide some answers to flesh out the text of my conspiracy theory in a later chapter.

WHAT WAS I LOOKING FOR?

At the interview when they ask, "what are your biggest weakness and your biggest strength?", rather than some smart-arsed answer, try this one. Tell them that you find it difficult to start something new, can make a small task last for ages, but, on the plus side, you have patience - the patience to wait 40 years for one of life's other "starters" to start putting useful stuff on the internet that you could adapt and put to good use.

My application was placed on the "smart-arsed" pile but I wasn't in any hurry. I mentioned previously that I had been looking for years for the name Spero Armorgie or any record of the existence of the name of Armorgie. I can confidently say that prior to 29 December 1871, the name Armorgie *never* existed. I have looked and never found any record of the surname - or even a plausible misspelling. To say that I have "looked" doesn't adequately describe the time and effort that others and I have put in over the years. Years? Decades would be more accurate.

The name Armorgie was actually made up. Of course, being pedantic, ALL names are effectively made up; how else would they come into existence? But, no, the name Armorgie was fabricated to cover the true identity of the man who was the father of an illegitimate child. That illegitimate child was Reginald Armorgie, my paternal great grandfather.

In family folklore, no one ever mentioned the fact that Reginald, son of Spero, was illegitimate nor even suggested it. Perish the thought! For with illegitimacy in those less enlightened times came some sort of perceived shame, suggesting that the family had not followed the rules. *Whose* rules we weren't following was never questioned but should have been questioned, for I have come to realise that in these matters we don't have to play by anyone else's rules. That's not to denigrate those rules, or rather those *social mores*, as they do establish codes of expected behaviour in a social group.

It is worth contextualising illegitimacy in the frame of it being in Victorian England. Unmarried mothers and their infants were considered an affront to morality and they were spurned and ostracised often by public relief as well charitable institutions. Moreover, it was recognised in the 19th century that illegitimate children were half as likely to survive compared to children with married parents, so it carried much more meaning than just having to bear the shame; it was about survival.

Someone or some people were colluding to help Louisa Crossley by covering for her being an unmarried mother, which she most certainly was. Again, I will later join the dots between Louisa's compromised condition and her place in the world; in someone else's world.

After that digression into the social history of Victorian England, I come back to explaining why I was looking for the real name of someone who had the alias Spero Armorgie. More than this, it became a question of how was I going to know when I *had* found him. I start to explain this in the next chapter.

Hunting for a man who was alive over 150 years ago, whose name I didn't know, and about whom I had no record, was apparently impossible. It wasn't even that I was looking for a needle in a haystack – I was first looking for the haystack and then, in the remote possibility that I should find it, I would have to sift through it to see if there was anything hidden that resembled a needle.

Ultimately it would come down to me feeling that I have learned enough from my search to feel satisfied that I have found an answer; deep down satisfied. What I did have in my favour was hope and determination.

WHO? WHAT? WHERE? WHEN? WHY?

There was an obvious question that puzzled me from even before I started my search for Spero: **Why** did no one previously know anything about the man that was Spero? Applying my cynical tendency, I reckoned that the truth *was* known, not widely known, but nevertheless known and covered up. The fact that nobody in the family knew anything tells me so much about *how*[7] he might have been part of Louisa's life, if not giving a clue to *who* he might have been. It was like he didn't want anyone to know and had something to hide. We all love a mystery or rather we like the answers to mysteries. Move over, Mr Holmes.

For me or anyone else wishing to find out more about him, a good approach seemed to be to think like Spero. Why did he choose to be the Man of Mystery? To answer that question I had to consider his very existence and to assume nothing. The latter was not difficult as I knew nothing. There was, however, an assumption borne out of the family wisdom handed down, and I had to step away from that. Let's face it, as a kid, if your dad tells you that he was the first man on the moon, it would take Junior Sceptic of the Year to dispute that fact.

---

[7] I would have put "how?" into the heading but it would have messed up my alliteration.

And so it was that I was led to believe that Spero was a Greek sailor. The name fitted, as did the fact that he came, he saw, he conquered. OK, so that was a Roman not a Greek. The thing is I could not accept as a *prima facie* case that Spero was a Greek or a sailor; as it turns out, he may well have had nautical tendencies. We live on an island so perhaps no surprise. And don't give me any old kebab shop argument to counter that, either.

In the simplest terms, someone called Spero was recorded as my great-great-grandfather. I have had to revisit the received understanding of who Spero Armorgie was. The question moved from "who was Spero?" to "**who** was my great-great-grandfather?" Subtly different but removing Spero's cloak that may be hiding something. Speculation is pointless but that has never stopped me from speculating as it creates the best stories.

What was Spero Armorgie and **what** did he have to hide? In social situations, what we "do" tends to define us but it says more about the person asking it than it does about the person expected to answer it.

The question is, "What do you do?", and it's usually asked by a man. Maybe women don't ask me as they know my answering style and they're in a hurry?

Of course, they want to know my occupation, my job, and, by association, my income and therefore my social status. There is an urge to want to put me a box, to reduce their subconscious feeling of being threatened by the unknown. In that fine, uptight English way, to enquire directly as to someone's job is considered somewhat vulgar. I suspect it has a throwback to the days when ennobled people, who often made the unwritten social rules, didn't always do what we would recognise today as work; servants and horses did that. On some old documents I have found, the man's occupation is referenced as being "gentleman".

One day, and it's not far off, I will respond to the whatdoyoudo? question with the reply that will indicate my

dislike of that question. I am still undecided between one of two replies;
1. "Fuck all" or,
2. "On Wednesdays I go shopping and have buttered scones for tea"

The exciting bit for me is in not knowing which truth will win the day. Maybe I might just modify my answer by a bit if it is the King asking this. QEII lost her opportunity to try it out on me.

Go on; ask me, I dare you.

So the question I had to answer was what did Spero "do" with his life? More significantly, what did he do such that he left no apparent footprints to tell us more about him, and why didn't he want us to know?

After exhausting my learning about the life of Reginald Armorgie, I had come to that metaphoric junction in the road of my search. The now well-documented life of my great grandfather would have been a satisfying end to my search for the origins of my surname, so much had I found. You will remember that I was travelling backwards in time and I had two routes that I planned to follow.

Where should I go next?

ROUTE 1 – DNA BROTHERS

The first route I took was encouraged by my extensive use of online ancestry research sites. Many of them offered ancestry research by DNA testing. I was a bit ignorant about exactly how it worked, but understood the basics of genetics and inheritance as I had been taught at school about Gregor Mendel's pioneering work. As far as I knew, Spero was not related to a pea plant but I thought I'd give it a shot.

The bit that was a mystery to me was how my DNA could be used to match to other people's and identify if or how I was possibly related, so whilst I waited for the results of my spitting into a test tube, I read a little more to understand what I might find. Again, it came with the warning to be prepared for what I might find, principally because there are options to learn if I was likely to be at risk of carrying some heritable health conditions. Other than that, the attraction was that I could expect to be given a list of other people who had tested and with whom I shared some DNA; my distant cousins basically. The results would indicate the geographic origins of my ancestors, and be accurate in matching as far back as about 5 generations or around 150-200 years. As Reginald Armorgie was born 86 years before me, I should apparently have inherited traceable amounts of his father Spero's DNA.

DNA evidence is a numbers game

An Englishman, a Welshman and an Irishman walk into a pub. The barman asks them, "Where's the Scotsman?"

One of the results of the analysis of my DNA is an ethnicity estimate. It came as no surprise to understand that my heritage is predominantly from the United Kingdom as shown in the table:

%	Maternal	Paternal	TOTAL
ENGLISH	27	0	27
IRISH	4	10	14
WELSH	6	28	34
SCOTTISH	12	10	22
Other	1	2	3
TOTAL	50	50	100

From conventional ancestry research I know the names of all 16 of my great great grandparents, but I only know the ethnic heritage of 15 of those. The exception was the star of the story, my paternal great great grandfather, Spero Armorgie. He is the enigma – but we've already established that.

Where I previously asked "who was Spero Armorgie?", I now qualify that to be "what was Spero Armorgie's real name?", the one that he was called at birth, and the surname that his son Reginald Armorgie *should* have inherited from his him – and, by extension, the one I *should* have inherited.

AMERICA'S HOPE

The results of my DNA test largely fitted my anticipated ethnicity but there were 2 surprises:
1. I had no English ethnicity on my father's side – so Spero was unlikely to have been of English stock
2. I had an estimated 10% Scottish ethnicity on my father's side – how so?

I should say that "English", in terms of genetic inheritance, is shorthand for saying that the ethnographic group may have been in England for centuries but may have come more generally in recent times to England from Belgium, northern France, Isle of Man, Luxembourg, Netherlands, Switzerland and the Channel Islands. This is because England has been a melting pot for various migrant groups throughout history, and continues to be so. Scottish, Welsh and Irish genes are identifiably separate from this English melange.

I have no knowledge of anyone whosoever on my father's side of the family with Scottish connections. In broad terms, 10% of my ethnicity would equate to me expecting to find that at least 1 of my 4 paternal great grandparents was Scottish or had Scottish parents, and therefore I should be invited to more New Year's Eve and Burns Night parties. *Slàinte mhath*!

There was also something in my DNA test results that 'scotched' the theory long held in Armorgie family folklore that Spero had been a Greek sailor. As I have indicated, he might well have been a sailor and he might possibly have sailed to Greece, but he was most unlikely to have descended from Greek heritage. If he had, I should have had more than an indication in my DNA test results.

Would I find Spero with DNA analysis? Would I expect to find him to be Scottish? I had the evidence and it was admittedly a long shot - but it was still a shot, and I was optimistic because I also had some other tools in my ancestry research toolbox to help narrow down which of my matches might be related to Spero.

That optimism is further buoyed by the hope that as more and more people perform DNA tests in future for family heritage research, there will be increasing possibilities of more matches. At the time I took my test, DNA testing had been around for a while but was still a relatively new tool for mass testing. Now pretty much every week I get new matches to people I am DNA related to. It is a growing pursuit and the evidence is amassing to prove, or disprove, what I think that I have found. My mind is open.

Before I leave this quick visit to the background of DNA testing, it is worth me not overlooking the 2% ethnicity of "other" in my paternal DNA breakdown. It is not actually just generic "other" on my paternal side; it is an estimate that I have DNA identified as originating from people from Germanic Europe. In this numbers game, the likelihood that Spero was from Germanic stock is 5 times less than him hailing from Scotland. Not probable but I did not discount the possibility…

You take the high road

From the results of my DNA numbers game I have a growing pool of people to whom I am DNA matched. They all share at least one common ancestor with me.

On the one website where I submitted my DNA test, it showed that I initially had 374 matches to other people who had also DNA tested and who were 4th cousins or closer. *What is a 4th cousin?* It is someone who shares a common great-great-great-grandparent. If I've got my maths and logic correct, and Mrs Davies agrees, in an even distribution and unbiased sample, I might expect to have about 23 of those 374 matches who had Spero's parents in their ancestry. Many of those matches had, like me, already constructed family trees from conventional, document

AMERICA'S HOPE

sources so I could see names of potential Spero candidates. The challenge was how I would know which of those names Spero's family name was. Mmm? It was tantalising to think that the name was probably there; all I had to do was find it <u>and</u> know with some degree of likelihood that I had found the right name. Is that *all*?

More than this scientific DNA evidence to help explain my heritage, I discovered one other key document. It's not your usual record of birth, marriage or death and the circumstances are something of a blessing in the context of me wanting to know. More on that unique document later.

I'll take the low road

Was I really looking for a Scotsman? Was the man identified as Spero actually resident in England in 1871? Was it Louisa who was actually elsewhere in 1871 when she conceived Reg? Why hadn't "Spero" married Louisa Crossley? These were questions I had to try to answer to focus my research and give me something I could believe.

I could narrow the search because, very fortunately, each of my 3 grandparents, away from my Armorgie paternal line, had a heritage from broadly different parts of the UK; one was from Wales, one was from Ireland, one was from England. When I was looking to narrow my search for those DNA matches who could share Spero's ancestry with me, I was potentially looking for someone with a higher estimate of Scottish ethnicity. This is how you start to eat an elephant; too big to eat in one go, so take it one bite at a time.

In case you were wondering how I progressed from an Englishman, a Welshman and an Irishman walking into a pub to ending up eating an elephant, you haven't seen the pub's lunch menu. You also possibly need to understand that I am covering up for not having a background in genetics. You guessed that. Now, however, after my DNA-based research in the Land of the Blind, you'll recognise me - I'm the one with the white stick being mocked by those elitists with one eye.

In case you were curious and hadn't noticed, probably not, I have to declare life experience in two areas of specialism; data analysis and cynicism. To the casual observer, these may appear to be mutually exclusive fields of expertise, yet they have served me well in my investigations. There is a possible 3rd area of expertise that can be explained if you remember what I said about my Dad - I may have unconsciously inherited his Bullshit Gene.

Even given the information that DNA analysis could provide, I accepted that it was likely that I may never *definitively* know the identity of Spero. All I could do was look at all the evidence and then make an evaluation. I was going to try to be dispassionate even though my heart had other ideas.

ROUTE 2 – BLOOD BROTHERS

The second route I took in my search for Spero was finding out more about the woman who was the mother of his child, my great great grandmother, Louisa Crossley. I was thinking that no one knows a son better than his mother. Her life will give me clues, if not the answer. As it turns out, neither of my chosen routes were the wrong route; they were complementary in leading me to my destination, or pretty close anyway.

Before I set off on this route, I will temper what I said about my experiences with the variety of spellings of the Armorgie surname through the ages. I have variously found the simpler name of Crossley spelled Crowsley, Crosley, Crofsley and Cropley. You're right, I won't let it go - I'll seethe all the way to my grave, and I don't think I have to worry about starting in the right place to find my way there.

The first piece of information that I knew about Louisa Crossley was that she had been in Bath for the birth of her son, Reginald. It certainly helps if a mother and her baby are in the same place when the baby is born. Being in Bath raised many questions that needed answers.

Where did she come from?
Where did she meet Spero?
Why did she not marry Spero?

Why did she move to Liverpool after the birth of Reg?
Did she get lost on her way to Bath?

Maybe this wasn't my Route 2, maybe it should be my Route 40 because Louisa was born in Leamington Spa, which, for the geographically challenged, is just off the M40 motorway between London and Birmingham. Yes, my 3 years of studying geography at university was a worthwhile investment in time; I've been waiting for this moment. With my already proven gift of hindsight, I should perhaps also have invested more time studying how to milk a joke out the M40 but, hey, I'm several chapters in and have pretty much exhausted that resource.

Louisa was born in 1845 in Royal Leamington Spa, to give it its full regal name which was granted following the patronage of Queen Victoria where she had visited the town as a Princess in 1830 and then as Queen in 1858. Every day is a school day. Louisa was the 6th of 11 children born to the family of Joseph Crossley, a carpenter, and his wife, Sarah.

I already mentioned Louisa staying in the home of her brother in Bath when she went there in 1871 to have her first child, my great grandfather, Reginald Armorgie. The previous record I had for Louisa was in 1861 when she was the live-in servant in the household of the Dale family in Leamington Spa. This was from the record from the 1861 Census of England and Wales, part of the ongoing census of UK citizens taken every 10 years.

Louisa would have been about a month pregnant with her baby, Reg, on the date of the next census, 2 April 1871. That census would be very revealing as to where she was, who she was with and what she was doing as an occupation. I did not expect to find the answer to the occupation question to be "On Wednesdays I go shopping and have buttered scones for tea". It would be unusual for her to have the manners that I appear to have adopted.

AMERICA'S HOPE

If my whole search for Spero wasn't one big mystery, this is one element of those unknowns that *still* remains a mystery. I have found no record where Louisa was on the date of the 1871 census. Was she even in the UK? Was she going by another name? The whole census has been digitised and is searchable, and I have searched it using every possible misspelling and possible pseudonym that I can think of, and more. Nothing. Hold this observation for later conspiracy testing.

After Reg's birth in Bath came Louisa's fairly swift movement back to Leamington with Baby Reg and then her marriage in January 1873 to William Long in Liverpool. I found the church record of Louisa and William's marriage in Liverpool and it indicates that both of them were working as servants and lived at the address of 19 Abercromby Square, Liverpool. I could have left it at that but clues are given to be followed – and I followed them.

At the time Louisa and William Long were married, their employer and residents in 19 Abercromby Square were Norman Stewart Walker, his wife Georgiana and their 5 children. In the 1871 census at that address, there was no record of either Louisa or William. The Walker parents were recorded as having been born in Virginia, USA, and were now naturalised British subjects. Living with them was Georgiana's widowed mother, also from Virginia, and one of their children had been born in Bermuda. Norman Walker's occupation was general merchant.

Six years later, the Longs, including Reginald, were living in Vine Street, Liverpool. There are records of them living at other addresses in Vine Street over the coming years. Reg lived with them at least until 1881, and shortly after made his excuses and left to start his short but unsuccessful career of helping himself to other people's money in West Yorkshire.

Louisa and William had 6 children together and when William died in 1900, Louisa was living with 4 of her children in Bloom Street, very close to where she had lived in Vine Street. Her eldest child was 25 years old and the youngest 8. She appears to have become a little forgetful about her date of birth. I would dearly like to think that she stayed in touch with Reg (when he was actually in England) and hope she got to meet her Armorgie grandchildren, all 3 of whom were born before she died in 1909, aged 63. In fact, her youngest child, Walter, was only 2 years older than her first grandchild, Alicia Armorgie. I would also like to know whether she took her secret to her grave with her or whether she had told anyone who Reg's father *really* was.

Louisa was living in her home in Vandyke Street, Liverpool, when she died. Louisa had managed to lose 6 years off her age on the 1900 census of England and Wales and she was on a roll, by the time she died, someone had been even more inventive and made her 10 years younger!

The house that was her home in Vandyke Street has also led a charmed life and is still standing today, if today is taken as an immovable concept. This is notable if, like me, one of your history reference sources is Willy Russell's musical play, *Blood Brothers*. This spoke (and sang) about much of the Victorian inner city homes in Liverpool being demolished in the 1950's and 1960's, and this included Louisa's old homes in Vine Street and Bloom Street. The residents would have been moved out to newly built overspill towns on the outskirts of Liverpool.

It looks like I haven't yet answered those questions that I originally posed about Louisa's life, and have even added some more things that I want to know about her. True to form, and unashamedly, I will fill in what I don't know with my conspiracy theory and you can be the judge about the plausibility - although I *did* learn from Louisa's life critical clues in my wider search for Spero. Actually, they were not so much about Louisa's life itself, but more specifically from the building in which she lived when she first moved to Liverpool and the building she lived in when working in Leamington Spa. There is a connection!

Before I knock on those particular doors, I'll leave you with my guess that, at some point later in time, Marilyn Monroe used to go dancing like Louisa Crossley.

THE WALLS HAVE EARS

19 Abercromby Square, where Louisa and William were living and working when they married, was a very different consideration to the houses that were in Vine Street and Bloom Street. It is a grand building on a grand square and is now a listed building, part of the University of Liverpool. It was built in 1862 by Charles Kuhn Prioleau, an American cotton merchant who became a naturalised British subject and was the senior partner of an American company who traded from an office in Liverpool.

19 Abercromby Square, Liverpool

Louisa and William Long were working at this address in the household of a wealthy merchant when they married. No surprises; that's what servants do. There were also no surprises that they were in Liverpool which, at that time, was prosperous and growing rapidly, as it became a world trade centre for general cargo and mass European emigration to the New World. There were jobs and opportunities and Louisa possibly came to Liverpool for those opportunities. I don't know if William Long and Louisa Crossley knew each other before they came to Liverpool. It seemed too much of a coincidence that William came from near Bath and Louisa had given birth to Reg in Bath just over a year prior to them marrying in Liverpool.

It was a long shot, not my first or last, but I wondered if 19 Abercromby Square held clues about Louisa's life that might point at who Spero was. There is a trope of a certain type of novel often referred to as a bodice ripper, and I'm not going there, but it was worth pursuing that line of investigation. Did Louisa have an affair with the gentleman of the house and have to make herself scarce when the consequences started to show? Be prepared for what you might find; I was warned!

My next exposure to being unprepared came from another quirk of fate in my life, or possibly ignorance in my life, which is harder to admit to than attributing it to fate. When I was at school, timetabling allowed me to choose to study to 'O' level (kids, ask your grandad) *either* geography *or* history. Given that I went on to study geography at university, guess which one I chose? The questions will get harder, I warn you. The upshot of my absence of a history 'O' level, or the (possible) embarrassing gap in my general knowledge, was that I did not know the dates of the American Civil War and, consequently, its possible implications on my life.

AMERICA'S HOPE

In fact, the consequence of me knowing bugger all about history was that it left a gaping hole in my general knowledge, and that acted as a speed bump on my route to finding out who was my great-great-grandfather. Is it possible to have a hole that's also a bump? It is if you mix your metaphors.

Oh, I should also admit to not having studied English beyond 'O' level. Does it show?

Big deal; I didn't know the dates of the American Civil War but then how could a war on another continent have any bearing on my life? I may not be good with dates but I had heard of the *butterfly effect*. In chaos theory, the butterfly effect is the sensitive dependence on initial conditions in which a small change in one place can result in large differences in another place. What that translates as, metaphorically, is that the formation and exact path taken by a tornado can be influenced by minor ripples such as a distant butterfly flapping its wings several weeks earlier. You knew that though.

Does it sound like I've lost the plot? I thought I had - but I found that I am better at jigsaw puzzles than I thought. The hard bit was finding all the pieces that had fallen down the back of the sofa.

I went looking for information about Norman Stewart Walker, Louisa Crossley's employer in Liverpool, not so much hidden in the sofa, but nevertheless a surprise. He had been a major in the Confederate Army and a Confederate States of America (CSA) Quartermaster agent during the civil war. He eventually became a naturalised British subject but he was a Virginian by birth. His father was born in Rothesay, Isle of Bute, Scotland.

Are you thinking now what I thought when I found out?

REALISATION

Ah.

BURDENS

"Burdens are for shoulders strong enough to carry them"

This is a quote from *Gone with the Wind*, written by Margaret Mitchell; another historical source of reference for me prior to this WTF Day #1. After that day, I decided to read a bit more widely.

Finding a possible family connection to a family who were movers and shakers in the Confederate States in the American Civil War was as much a shock as finding an Armorgie with connections to The Daily Mail. As a child, my only knowledge about the Southern Confederate legacy was what I learned watching *The Dukes of Hazzard*[8]. Yes, I may joke and I know for many that the issues around what was fought for in the Civil War are very sensitive, but I do not make jokes that in any way are meant to be disrespectful. I may have wandered into the DMZ of joke making so I know I've only got myself to blame for any consequences.

I also appreciate that there is a masking romanticism of the Deep South; the plantations, sitting on the porch drinking mint juleps, peach cobbler in the oven, *Gone with*

---

[8] The usual caveat about asking parents applies here.

the Wind, and so on. These images are a far cry from the equally very real association with visceral, racial slavery. As I sought to understand the world that was portrayed as Tara or Hazzard County, I also learned how it related to Liverpool.

Liverpool had, and still has, definite links with the Confederate cause; I learned that, for years, Confederate sympathisers have come to Liverpool to remember this part of their heritage. It largely passes under the radar but now, in the wake of the global Black Lives Matter protests, the city is reconsidering the symbols of that part of its past, and working out how to use them to educate Liverpool's future generations. I very much do not want to cause or perpetuate any divisions – far from it, I hope that my personal story does for others what it has done for me in helping me understand. Liverpool has had more than its fair share of division.

To keep this in context, my story does more than touch on the issue of race; it has other potentially sensitive issues of gender, privilege, morality and others to which I may be blind. I am not going out of my way to avoid writing about anything sensitive yet neither am I raising any issues just for the sake of controversy. I am aware of people's sensibilities but I will not adding to the list that begins, "Rain drops on roses and whiskers on kittens…" – although I will continue to draw humour out of it; such is my way.

Here's a test, your starter for 10, what were the dates of the American Civil war? No, I thought as much; I'll tell you. It started on 12 April 1861, and *officially* ended on 9 April 1865. I say officially as there is an even less well known post-script to that end date. The last shot of the Civil War was fired from Confederate States Ship (CSS) *Shenandoah* in June 1865, and this ship was the last military unit of the Confederate States to surrender. That last surrender was made on 6 November, 1865, in the River Mersey, off the port of Liverpool, made to the captain of HMS Donegal.

AMERICA'S HOPE

CSS Shenandoah

This surrender of the *Shenandoah* was nearly 7 months after the end of the war because its captain, James Iredell Waddell, and his crew were unaware of the Confederate States' surrender, given the means of ship to shore communications at that time. They learned of the surrender on 3 August 1865 when they encountered a British barque in the Bering Sea where *Shenandoah* was raiding American whalers. Captain Waddell feared that returning to a port in the USA and surrendering to US federal authorities would run the risk of him and his crew being tried in a US court and hanged as pirates, so he decided to surrender his ship in the port of Liverpool. He knew that Confederate Commander James Dunwoody Bulloch was stationed in Liverpool, in a country where he thought he might receive leniency. It was a long journey from the Bering Sea, all the way south down the eastern Pacific Ocean, around Cape Horn, through the south Atlantic and north Atlantic, back to the UK. I say *back* to the UK as the *Shenandoah* had been built in Scotland and originally sailed from London after being bought by the Confederate States.

COLIN ARMORGIE

Roosevelt link with Liverpool

**Theodore "Teddy" Roosevelt (L) and
Jefferson Davis (R)**

Liverpool's links to America were so much more entrenched at the time my great great grandmother was living and working there. James Dunwoody Bulloch was the uncle of future US President, Theodore "Teddy" Roosevelt, who was a visitor to the city. Whilst I was investigating this and the wider part that Liverpool played in US history I also found that Jefferson Davis had a connection to Liverpool. Jefferson Davis was President of the Confederate States and his connection to Roosevelt in Liverpool was surprising.

The young Teddy Roosevelt was a visitor to Liverpool in 1869 and 1870, arriving with his parents at the age of 10 for a European tour. In his diary entry of 27 May 1869, he wrote, "went to our cousin's school at Waterloo. We had a nice time, but met Jeff Davises son and some sharp words ensued."

Fight!

AMERICA'S HOPE

Waterloo is a suburb of Liverpool, and I will later explain why not only one, but two, of Theodore Roosevelt's uncles were in Liverpool, why they were part of the exiled Confederate community in that city, and why Jefferson Davis and his family were there. Sometimes if I tell others something that I know about, it can sound quite patronising, so for now I will be modest and simply say that in this matter I am a fucking expert. If you think I'm making it up, do your own research and stop depending on me.

The connections of these Americans to Liverpool and the connections of my family to these Americans was much of the reason I kept on searching for my heritage. On the face of it, my chance of finding out was more remote than me finding my way to Bath on a unicycle whilst wearing a blindfold[9]. What it did give me was a rich source of documented history that was at worst interesting, and at best, gave me the possibility of me actually finding the true identity of Spero Armorgie.

---

[9] Believe me, I could do it – as long as I started in the right place.

LEAMINGTON SPA

I was captivated by reading the story of the *Shenandoah* and its appointment with destiny in Liverpool, and the apparent craziness of this made me now unwilling to dismiss any line of possible information that might lead to Spero Armorgie. While reading more about the history of the *Shenandoah* I found a photograph taken in Leamington Spa in 1865 of 5 of the former officers who had served on the *Shenandoah*. Leamington Spa – how so? You will remember this is the town in which Louisa Crossley was born. Curiouser and curiouser. I was on the case!

At that time, the population of Leamington Spa was about 20,000. Why would exiles from the Confederate States not return to post-war USA and instead gravitate to a small town in a rural part of England, away from the coast? The first thing to understand was that there were certain people who were not included in the terms of the Amnesty Proclamation of the US president at the close of the Civil War. This included "all parties who have been engaged in the destruction of the commerce of the United States upon the high seas", which covered the Americans of the crew of the *Shenandoah*.

COLIN ARMORGIE

Former crewmen of CSS Shenandoah in Leamington 1865, which shows Assistant Surgeon, Edwin G. Booth (seated), and (standing, left to right): Acting Master Irvine S. Bulloch, Passed Assistant Surgeon, Bennett W. Green, First Lieutenant, William H. Murdaugh, and Passed Assistant Surgeon Charles E. Lining.

At that time in Leamington Spa there was a small community of Confederate expatriates. Those *Shenandoah* officers were there to visit their own folk. The Confederate exiles in Leamington Spa were there principally because the Amnesty Proclamation also excluded those whose personal property exceeded $20,000. These people possessed vast fortunes, or at least they did before the Civil War. That Confederate community included those who were merchants, cotton traders, plantation owners and therefore also possibly slave owners. Many of them had also financed the Confederate war effort from the UK. Some of them

AMERICA'S HOPE

were also excluded from returning to the United States for double, triple and even quadruple whammies present in the Amnesty Proclamation because they:

- Were absentees from the United States for the purpose of aiding the rebellion, and/or
- Had resigned or tendered resignations of their commissions in the army or navy of the United States, and/or
- Had been military or naval officers of the 'pretended' Confederate Government above the rank of Colonel in the army or Lieutenant in the navy

They really were not immediately welcome back in the USA, so sleepy Leamington Spa must have looked quite attractive by comparison to prison, or worse, in America. The restrictions of the amnesty were eventually relaxed and most exiles drifted 'home' in the 1870s, although home would now look a lot different to them; I had seen Atlanta burning in the closing scenes from *Gone with the Wind*. Any quote you need about this, you can provide for yourself, frankly, my dear.

I found an article describing life in the "the little nest of Confederates in Leamington". This was taken from the diary of Mrs. Georgiana Walker, the wife of Major Norman Walker, the Confederate agent in Bermuda. This was WTF Day #2. The Walkers were Louisa Crossley's employers at the time she married in Liverpool in 1873.

This article referred to Mrs. Walker arriving in Leamington Spa with her four children in early July 1864, where they found accommodation, first at **22 Dale Street**, then at 60 Portland Street. In 1861 Louisa Crossley was living and working as a servant at **5 Portland Road**, Leamington Spa. I have yet to find reference to Louisa working for the Walkers in Leamington but I think it would be more unusual had Louisa *not* known them in some way in Leamington Spa.

I found in Leamington's documented history this paragraph:

"*Most Confederate families lived in what is still a pleasant residential area, to the north-west of the town centre, comprising **Portland Road, Dale Street** and Grove Street, with one or two more in Lansdowne Crescent, to the north-east.*"

The Walkers were not in Leamington Spa for very long (this time) and left on 30 September 1864, bound for Halifax, Nova Scotia, where Major Walker was to resume his operations as purchasing agent for the Confederates. In January 1865 they relocated back to Bermuda where they were resident when the American Civil War ended on 9 April 1865. On 13 May, they left Bermuda bound for England again. Guess where they settled? If you guessed Leamington Spa, you'd be correct. I'm making this too easy for you.

The former Confederate President, Jefferson Davis, was imprisoned in the USA at the end of the war, and when he was released in May 1867, Davis travelled to Europe with his wife, Varina, to recuperate and seek opportunities that would not be afforded to him the USA. For approximately six weeks, beginning on 9 November 1868, the Davis family resided in Leamington Spa. The Walkers were no longer in Leamington Spa at that time, because they left Leamington Spa in February 1866 and moved to London.

The Walkers moved from London to Liverpool in 1867, initially to a house Napier Terrace, Canning Street, only a few hundred yards from Abercromby Square, and then to 19 Abercromby Square in 1870. Norman Walker started a cotton importing business with his father-in-law, Thomas Gholson. I previously mentioned a quote attributed to Georgiana Walker's personal diary and I tracked down and bought a copy of Georgiana Walker's diary at a bookshop in California. In that diary it reveals that while they were in Liverpool, the Walkers hosted the Davises on several visits in the years following the war, between 1867 and 1874.

What I was most interested in finding in Georgiana Walker's diary was any reference to Louisa being in their household, or any "events" involving her that were more than just her employment and residency. I was shocked by what I read – not by the absence of any reference to Louisa but by Georgiana's language that can euphemistically described as "from a different time". I was not reading this to stand in judgement but it is hard not to, and I realise that my judgement of it being shocking is based on the set of rules and expectations that govern us today. Georgiana was the very image of a stereotype of a Southern Lady but underneath that outward elegance and refinement was the brutal ugliness of racism, and this showed in what she wrote. Her family and Norman's had been plantation owners before the war and, almost by default, had been slave owners.

It was at this point I wondered why a well-connected, wealthy southern family, exiled to a foreign land, cushioned by their wealth, should have employed Louisa Crossley. The Walkers had been slave owners, and therefore possibly not top of the list of people known for benevolence to their servants. I am sure they could have picked and chosen whichever staff suited the appearance that they wanted their English household to make to their society and to their guests. I already described the Victorian era in England being one where illegitimate mothers were typically spurned and ostracised, so why then would the Walkers have employed, and had living under their roof at 19 Abercromby Square, Louisa Crossley, an unmarried young mother?

As part of my conspiracy theory, I can make a good case for the Walkers in some way being complicit with Louisa's condition, or that they somehow felt responsible. I'll ask Stormy Daniels how it works.

There is much to read on the internet about the history of Abercromby Square and number 19 in particular. Charles

COLIN ARMORGIE

Prioleau, who had commissioned the building of number 19, was a member of a group called *The Southern Club*. Now, as everyone knows, Liverpool is famous for being the home of many famous and popular music venues, but *The Southern Club* wasn't one of those. Neither was it an entertainment venue with a dance floor, lightshow, a stage for live music and a DJ. That was the *Cavern Club*.

The *Liverpool Southern Club* was formed in 1862 and drew its membership from among highly influential businessmen who hailed from the American southern states who settled in Liverpool, like Charles Prioleau. They were involved in creating and managing trade networks between the Confederate States of America and Britain. The Confederates wanted European political allies and the British Government remained outwardly neutral, but this didn't stop the Confederates buying uniforms, weapons, ammunition and ships – nor did it stop some Liverpool manufacturers and merchants getting very rich from this trade. The politics were far more complicated than I need to convey here, save to say that Louisa Crossley had worked for a Confederate family – and I had to determine if my great great grandfather was a Confederate. "Had to"? Of course, I didn't *have to* but I'd had 60 plus years of not knowing and I know that not knowing is worse than knowing. Yeah, I know that you know that I'm a don't-know-it-all; I previously mentioned my talent as a KIA but failed to say it left me as I got older.

At the outbreak of the Civil War, Liverpool showed alliance with the Confederates through the press and by public gatherings, however, the alliance was most prominent through the original intention of 19 Abercromby Square being an unofficial embassy in Liverpool for the Confederacy, providing a base for business and diplomacy. Although there is no direct proof of this claim, according to a contemporary newspaper account at that time, Number 19 was specifically designed to be a "European White

House" for the Confederate President Jefferson Davis - if the South had been victorious.

Having learned the basics of Liverpool's and Leamington's association with the Confederate States, I was very tempted to join the dots between Louisa's mystery pregnancy and the fact that about that time she had been living and working in the home of a Confederate merchant in Liverpool. There was, however, still the matter of over 6 years of disconnect between the end of the Civil War and the birth of Reginald Armorgie, and I also wasn't intending to just add another plausible yet vague, unsubstantiated circumstantial theory to the Greek sailor theory.

I wanted some sort of evidence.

NORMAN STEWART WALKER

The family of Norman Stewart Walker next fell under my spotlight, as they were Louisa Crossley's employer at the time she married and also had connections to Louisa's home town of Leamington Spa. I said that 19 Abercromby Square had a story to tell and it was certainly the best lead that I had tracing back from the information I found about her marriage.

In the same way that I didn't want to make an unsubstantiated connection to Spero having any involvement in the American Civil War, I also didn't want to point the finger of paternity without evidence. Let me first deal with things that I *did* find, things that relate to the circumstances of the Walkers and Liverpool during the Civil War, things that are interesting and things that may hold clues.

Norman Walker's operation as CSA Quartermaster required the services of ships willing to undertake the journey from Liverpool and also, particularly, from the entrepôts in places like Cuba, Bermuda and Canada. The goods from Europe having crossed the North Atlantic Ocean had to be loaded onto smaller ships with a shallower draught to enter the shallower waters of the Confederate ports, and this reloading happened in those ports in neutral waters. Norman Walker conducted most of his activity during the Civil War from Bermuda.

This wartime supply operation required ships' captains and crews willing to undertake the journey running through the Union naval blockade of the ports of the southern states. It was a very lucrative trade to those seamen who chose to do it but it was also very dangerous. These ships were referred to as blockade runners. Rhett Butler, the character played by Clark Gable in *Gone with the Wind*, was said to have earned his wealth and influence as a blockade runner. I am perhaps overworking the relevance of this film as a source of historical information but bear with me; it will have a later significance.

By some strange inter-weaving of circumstance, 19 Abercromby Square played a further role in the chequered Armorgie heritage; it is pure coincidence but spookily notable, nevertheless. Roll forward the history of Number 19 from the Walker's residence to 1877, when it was leased out by Norman Walker on a five-year contract, apparently to help with his struggling finances. Of no apparent connection to Spero (but, hey, you never know!) the Haitian Ambassador to Liverpool took up residence at Number 19. In 1882, the Walker's finances were not improving, and so Number 19 was sold. The City of Liverpool later purchased Number 19 in 1882 and transformed it into the Bishop's Palace for the first Bishop of Liverpool. Then, in the 1920s, 19 Abercromby Square became part of the University of Liverpool, to whom it belongs today.

Unlike my parents and brothers, my cousin, Phil Armorgie, wasn't forced into southern exile in Surrey, England; well, not immediately. He was brought up in Liverpool until he eventually got appointed to the role of Liverpool's Cultural Ambassador to Windsor – Windsor the town, not the Royal Palace. When I told Phil of the Armorgie-Abercromby Square connection, he recalled that his aunt, on his mother's side, had worked in Number 19 in the 1970s, in its current incarnation as part of the University of Liverpool. I am going to make representations to Liverpool City Council to ask that that this building be established as the Armorgie White House, such are our family connections to it.

The crucial question for me was whether 19 Abercromby Square was holding any secrets that might indicate Reginald Armorgie's paternity. Leaping forward to the present day, I searched for any clues in my DNA test results that might show a connection to the Walker family. What I found was quite the opposite but was necessarily quite informative. I found the genealogical research of Chip Lewis in the USA, and he is great grandson of Norman Stewart Walker. Chip is another who has taken a DNA test and whose results are loaded to the same website as mine, and we have concluded that there is <u>no</u> genetic connection shown between Chip and me. If I were descended from Norman Stewart Walker or his sons, then there would have been a DNA match between Chip and me.

IT WON'T HAPPEN TO ME

Scientists have suggested that humans are generally wired by evolution to naturally see their glass as half full. To give it some fancy words and add credence to this latest of my little diversions, it has been called *Optimism Bias*; a cognitive bias that causes some people to believe that they themselves are less likely to experience a negative event.

It won't happen to me and, if it does, I can deal with it; that's it in a nutshell.

This attitude is based on a general knowledge about the world gathered from learned experiences. This is how young people typically know it all and, as they grow older, strangely lose that knowledge. How does that happen? I am unable to answer my own question as I have lost that knowledge.

There is another explanation to those who ignore warnings, like the vague warning I had received, "Be prepared for what you might find". Stupidity is the explanation. The odds are easily misjudged even though the warning signs are there. My simple preparation for dealing with unforeseen difficulties that I might turn up in my family history was to disclaim any personal connection to the past. Simple. I realised that with that approach I actually *could* fool some of the people all the time and all of the people some of the time, however, I couldn't fool myself any of the time. That was hard.

Of course, I had potential coping mechanisms available to me, things like the well-honed past tactics of my mother's family, which involved avoiding finding out the truth and, failing that, not telling anyone. I carried on my research and, well, here I am telling anyone who cares to read. If I am to extend the original literary allusion of this being my "quest", I feel a bit like the *Ancient Mariner*, forced to spend eternity repeating my story, searching for the person who actually understands what my quest has meant to me.

"'There was a ship,' quoth he."

"Actually, lad, there were quite few ships, all made by the scouse shipwrights of Birkenhead[10]." To appease those who don't like to see literature being desecrated, I will admit that I have put my spin on that quote.

On more than one level, I seek no forgiveness – except for my digression in telling my story.

When I said that I was shamefully ignorant about the dates of the American Civil War, I very much **did** know the politics behind the reasons for that war. I can't hope to cover it all here and neither should I, but I also can't ignore that not everyone is aware. It is necessary to set the context of what I have found and am writing about.

In a very condensed form, there were longstanding tensions and disagreements between the northern states in America and seven southern states. These were related to economic policies, cultural values, the extent and reach of the federal government, and the role of slavery within American society. The seven southern "slave states"

---

[10] Geosocial Note: Birkenhead is on the opposite bank of the River Mersey to Liverpool and the people who live there are apparently fed up of all the jokes that the people of Liverpool tell about them. I was born close to there and I'm not bitter.

seceded from the Union and formed a new nation, the Confederate States of America.

Of course, slavery was the most prominent area of disagreement. Some may disagree; that's why I will demur from delving into the more distant events in history. To round off this context-setting, I will add that in 1807 the slave trade was abolished by Act of Parliament in Great Britain.

What did affect me were the more recent related events in world history running in parallel with what I was finding in my family history. On 7 June 2020, in my home town of Bristol, the statue of Edward Colston was toppled, defaced, and pushed into the harbour during the wider protests about the death of George Floyd in Minneapolis, USA. This was related to the *Black Lives Matter* movement that had been growing across the world since 2013.

Edward Colston had been born in Bristol and was an English merchant, slave trader, philanthropist, and Tory Member of Parliament. It is not surprising that the anger of the crowd was not really triggered by his ventures as a merchant, a philanthropist or a Tory MP.

At that same time, in the same climate of awareness, Liverpool was similarly and publicly facing up to its historical role in the Atlantic slave trade. Public apologies, marches and toppling statues is a very British way of protesting. You know where I'm going: Trans-Atlantic. The Americans weren't going to be out-demonstrated by the Limeys.

In America, the battle flag of the Confederate States is still revered by some, particularly in the south, but to others it is widely still seen as a symbol of slavery that should have been consigned to history with abolition in the USA. It is a symbol division. Civil War is the ultimate embodiment of division.

I am going to introduce someone to the story who is hopefully more recognisable than Gentleman Farmer, and someone who doesn't need a biog like Edward Colston. Stop me if you haven't heard of Donald J. Trump. Events around the end of Trump's presidency reignited the debate over the continued flying of the Confederate flag – if the debate, in fact, had ever been extinguished.

On 6 January 2021, following the defeat of US President Donald Trump in the 2020 presidential election, a mob of his supporters attacked the United States' Capitol Building in Washington, DC. Some of those rioters carried Confederate battle flags and for the first time in US history, a Confederate battle flag was displayed inside the Capitol.

Donald has left the building but the ghosts of confederacy haven't, and they have also entered my conscience. I have to deal with it. These events formed the untimely backdrop to my investigations into my family history.

INFERENCE-OBSERVATION CONFUSION

As human beings we suffer from an innate tendency to jump to conclusions; to judge people too quickly and to pronounce them failures or heroes without due consideration of the actual facts and ideals of the period.
King Charles III of Gracelands[11]

Yes, the psychological term for jumping to conclusions is "inference-observation confusion".

In my search for Spero I was also keenly aware that I might apply *celebrity* cognitive bias in my investigation strategy. The pool of people I could research included many historically significant, high profile people, affluent, politically exposed people, whose lives were consequently well documented. Of course, there was more reason that Spero could have been an "also-ran" in this slice of history that I was investigating; a sailor on a Confederate ship, a servant in the household of an American family, anyone from the melting pot that was boom-time Liverpool - simply someone more ordinary. I was cautious and needed

---

[11] To keep you on your toes, that's the punchline of a later joke. When you find the joke come back here and email me the laugh.

to not only be convinced by the evidence but to convince myself that the evidence was believable.

To relieve the boredom faced by so many during lockdown in the UK during the Covid-19 pandemic, I made a number of revelations to my family about what I was finding in my family tree research. The great advantage was that using cloud-based video conferencing I could bludgeon them with blunt PowerPoint presentation and simultaneously mute the sound. There was no dissension and, I daresay, not much relief of boredom.

I realise that prematurely voicing my suspicions about Spero's identity led to me wearing out my credibility quota. I have this suspicion that if I now tell an Armorgie that it's raining, they will go to look out of the window just to check; twice probably, just to make sure. In terms of the paternity of Reg Armorgie, I pointed the finger first at someone in the Walker household in Liverpool and, successively, at various others. Maybe I showed my cards too early. I will give the context in an analogy that Armorgies will understand.

In the 2005 UEFA Champions League final in Istanbul, Liverpool FC were losing 3-0 to AC Milan at half time. The players had belief and Liverpool went on to bring home from Istanbul their 5th European Cup. I am not going to parade this book through the streets of Liverpool on an open-top bus but I would urge a bit of belief.

I may be channelling the spirit of my father by not letting facts get in the way of a good story or four, but I now have the self-conviction that I now have a Spero candidate that I can reveal and won't later come to regret. How did I find him?

TRUSTING TO LUCK IS NOT A STRATEGY

If I had resigned myself to just accumulating information about the history of my known family, it would have been very satisfying to add detail to what I already knew. However, I wanted to look beyond that, beyond the born-married-died and into what I referred to as *known unknowns*. I needed to shape a strategy; I needed to write my own history.

Was I convinced that Spero was a man from the Confederate community in the Civil War? No, but I needed to put down some markers in an attempt to find my great great grandfather, a man whose name I was convinced that I didn't know. It did not seem unreasonable for me to use the clues in Louisa Crossley's life and take a punt on the Civil War Confederate connection; these were my *known knowns*. I took various threads to shape a strategy...

Was he in Liverpool in 1871?

Or was he possibly in Leamington Spa – or both? This is on the assumption that Louisa was the one who remained there whilst the other players entered stage left and departed stage right. I had certain pieces of information to help establish this, most notably the diary of Georgiana Walker. I also had the dates on my side, too. There was a census of people in England, Wales and Scotland on 2 April 1871, the year that Reginald Armorgie was conceived and born, and the names of people in those census records can be searched online. Strangely the Irish census returns for that year were destroyed by the government after the statistical information about the population had been collated. I have nothing but love for Ireland, particularly given my pedigree, but in this context I hoped that Spero wasn't Irish.

There was a census taken in the USA on 1 June 1870, so that would also give me a good idea of any American exiles and ex-patriots in Britain who had returned home after the Civil War period. Of course, it didn't mean that Americans weren't crossing the Atlantic to the UK at any time before or after having been enumerated on that census, but it was nevertheless a good clue.

As an aside, it was a strange reality in looking at the 1870 US Census and finding records of men who had played significant roles in the Civil War on both sides, who had been heroic, selfless and daring, and who had now joined the new, peacetime American society in roles such as farmers, lawyers and, very common, insurance salesmen! None of these occupations are in any way unworthy; they just feel so very different to the lives they lived during war time. Well, they felt so different to my experience given that I had never been required to fight for my country, and I hope I never have to.

There are also many books that have been written about the fate of men involved in the American Civil War, and these are sources of historically relevant information. I say *historically relevant* rather than *historical sources* of information because I am very aware of the potential for historical inaccuracies in *my* story, or should I say possible economies of truth, or having had a filter applied to allow me to select just the corroborating evidence. Surely not? This puts me in a Catch-22 situation because if I deny participating in any such skulduggery, it might look like I am overly protesting my innocence, yet if I don't deny it, it might look like I am pleading the Fifth Amendment[12].

I could be making up this whole story; it will be interesting to see whether those who make these judgements will categorise this book as fiction or non-fiction.

Was he American?

This was never a "given" and is a concept that is a little nebulous. There were people who lived in America who had not taken American citizenship, there were Britons who fought in the American Civil War, there were American citizens who became naturalised British citizens, and there were Americans who had immigrated to the United States who were culturally still aligned to their native country. My reference to "American" covers it quite nicely as a broad indicator in respect of my search.

Was he associated with the Confederate cause?

This would be a big clue but, of course, it wouldn't be definitive.

Gender

Of course, my great great grandfather had to be a bloke; I don't need to go into the mechanics but it's simply how it works with paternal lineage. True, although as it turned out, a big clue to me identifying my prime Spero suspect was associated with a woman who has yet to enter my story.

---

[12] That reference may come from my American blood (to be confirmed)

Confused? I will keep my musket and powder dry, thoroughly mix my metaphors and spill the beans later.

Is there evidence of any DNA connection?

From the DNA test that I took, the results show people to whom I am genetically related. I looked at the family trees of these people to see if they contained any of the names I was aware of from other sources. Similarly, and in more detail, where I did find a likely paternal DNA connection, did it point to someone with a Scottish heritage? As I previously identified, I have a strong indication that my missing paternal line had Scottish origins.

In the absence of a known name for my paternal great great grandfather, other than the pseudonym Spero Armorgie, DNA connection to someone who fitted the other criteria would present the strongest evidence of who he might be.

Age

It might be expected to find "Spero" was the same sort of age as Louisa in 1871. I don't have an exact birth date for Louisa but I know that her birth was registered in quarter 4 1845 so would have probably have been aged 26 when Reg was born.

Appearance

I have just one photograph of Reg Armorgie and would expect some similarity to anyone otherwise suspected of being Spero Armorgie, his father. This is always supposing that I can find a photograph of any Spero candidate, and is also potentially masked by the fact that I have no photograph of Louisa Crossley / Long. How much did Reg take after his father and how much after his mother?

AMERICA'S HOPE

Fingers crossed

The odds were against me; I had no guarantee of success so a little luck would have been a great help in my search strategy. And so it came to pass.

PROBABILITY OF SUCCESS

I realise now that the success or otherwise of my search strategy was never going to be a simple box ticking exercise; there was going to be a large element of subjectivity. Even given the hard information that DNA analysis can provide, I am resigned to the thought that it is unlikely that I will 100% definitively know the identity of Spero. I have accepted this and also accepted that I had to take a pragmatic approach. I would look at the evidence and then make an evaluation.

For me, no amount of certainty would be an end to my search but just a continuation of my exploration. When or if I think I have found out *who* Spero was, I will want to know *what* he was, *where* he was, *why* he was there and, more particularly, *why* he remained anonymous and *why* he then disappeared. My search will, of course, be time limited.

How do I know that I will probably never truly know the identity of the man who was my great-great-grandfather? Well, given the richness of available resources and the time that I have spent searching, I would have expected to have found the definitive answer by now. The clues were out there and I have found some of them, although I like to think that they haven't all yet been found.

I do feel that I have found sufficient to give me something, and that something may be enough.

Ultimately, "enough" comes down to me feeling that I have learned enough from my search to feel satisfied that I have found the answer; the *deep down satisfied* I mentioned previously, in my heart as much as in my head.

Additionally, as important as it is for me to look at the evidence and make my evaluation, it is for anyone else who is interested to also look at the evidence and to make up their own mind for themselves.

"SUSPICION OFTEN CREATES WHAT IT SUSPECTS"

No, this chapter heading is nothing I read on a fridge magnet, it is another quote by C. S. Lewis, and it reminded me that I ought to be dispassionate in my search for Spero. It is hard to be dispassionate when you've got a genetic connection and a spiritual connection. Whilst delving into Liverpool's Confederate history I found lots of colourful characters who could make it onto my casting shortlist of candidates to be selected to play Spero in Liverpool's version of *Gone with the Wind*, not all of them of the right moral character. The Wiki entry for the character Rhett Butler is described as him having a personality is that of a "cynical, charming, and mocking philanderer". Mmm?

To give an idea of the scale of my investigation, I researched the lives of about 60 men who I classed as "Liverpool Americans" from the civil war period and the years following, and I applied the filters to seek a potential match – did I have any evidence of a DNA connection to anyone who is known to be related to them? Were they in Liverpool in 1871? And so on. The results were not as instant as I could have hoped for.

It is worth putting some scale of time and effort that I spent on this. I had been looking for Spero for 35 years but it wasn't proper research; the odd trip to Bath, talking about it around the dinner table, looking at family history documents held by the family, a visit to St Catherine's House[13] in London, etc. It was a search of sorts, but not concerted. The identification and investigation of the 60 men in my short list took the best part of two and a half years concerted effort, pretty much daily, with the wall of my office ending up like a crime scene investigation. There was too much to hold in my head; I had, have, over 12,000 people in my database from which I sifted the 60 candidates. For all that this is not written to be a handbook on *How to Find Your Great Great Grandfather*, I will go on to explain later how this was achieved. I should "show my workings" as Mrs Davies would have expected. It may also make me look pretty smart – you can choose your own expression for my vanity.

Having built this pool of names, it required a massive amount of curation of details, principally using the tools available on ancestry websites and, resorting to my comfort zone of using spreadsheets and a Ouija board. Don't judge me adversely. I went down countless rabbit holes but I got a result that I was surprisingly happy to find. That is I was surprised I found anything and I was happy to have found it. The ends justified the means.

Actually, my admitted use of spreadsheets is true but the use of a Ouija board isn't. Maybe I shouldn't have been so blinkered but if I had based the proof of my investigation on communicating with the dead, there might have been some sceptics who would not believe the results; living sceptics only.

Of course, I did not lose sight of the great possibility that Spero Armorgie did not come from this category of Liverpool Americans, however, if I had found no

---

[13] The office of the Registrar General of Births, Marriages and Deaths for England and Wales, after it moved from nearby Somerset House, which was a byword in older generations for family records held by the state.

connection, you could rightly guess I wouldn't be writing this. You're smart, you are.

TWO'S COMPANY, THREE'S A CROWD

If the results of my DNA tests shows me genetically connected to two different people, and their family trees show that they have the same common, shared ancestor, then there is a fair probability that I might share that same common ancestor. Those two people and their shared ancestor form a triangle when drawn in a family tree, and this is known as triangulation – and that's not just me being obtuse.

Don't worry if that doesn't make sense, as it won't prevent any understanding when it comes to the big reveal. It's just me showing my workings again.

This triangulation was the basis for my use of my DNA test results to demonstrate a possible connection to an ancestor that I had no other record of being related to. Of course, there is no guarantee that I share the common ancestor in any triangulation but it is a good starting point to investigate the shared ancestry and look for Liverpool American links.

When I found the first triangle, I thought that's it, Spero has been outed! The reality was less clear. To date I have found 332 people with whom I share a previously unknown common ancestor. In fact, I have found hundreds more than that but I have discounted the ones where I can identify the lineage of the connection back to my maternal ancestors or down the non-Armorgie paternal line.

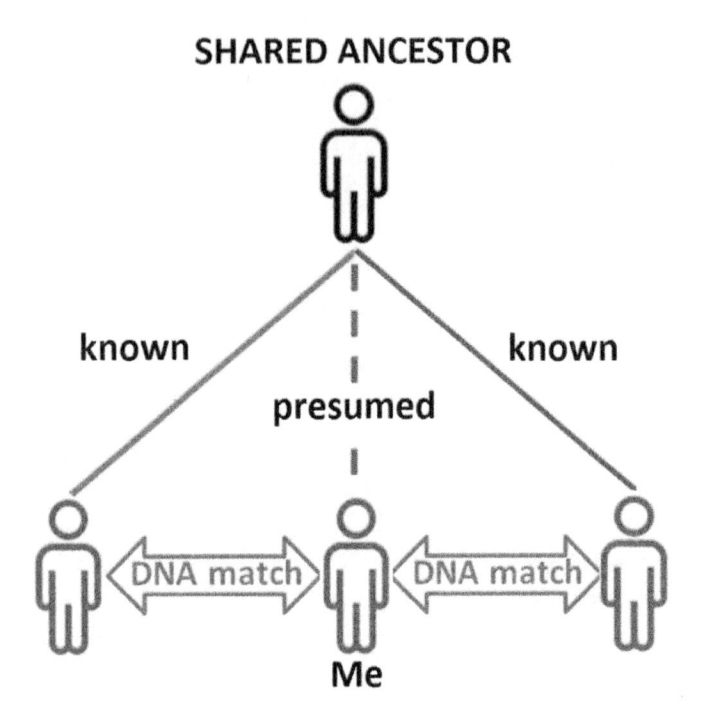

SHARED ANCESTOR

known / presumed / known

DNA match — Me — DNA match

This is one of the reasons that my search has taken so long since I took my DNA test. Those 332 DNA matches are only the ones who *could* share the same DNA that I share with Spero Armorgie.

Amongst those 332 there are cases where more than two of them (and me, hopefully) share the same common ancestor. Also amongst those 332 there was a majority who had American ancestry that traced back to the United Kingdom. I couldn't read too much into these broad findings because ancestry research using DNA testing is much more prevalent in the USA than all other countries.

Similarly, I would expect to find people who had the same ethnicity as me which is 99% from the British Isles.

I've thrown many numbers into my numbers game and will summarise the key figures. I have over 12,000 people in my "Spero database" and 332 of those are people I am DNA related to. Separately I had a record of 60 known "Liverpool Americans". In my wordy equivalent of a Venn diagram, I now had to see if any of these 60 men were amongst the men who I had identified as shared, common ancestors.

I initially narrowed the "Liverpool American shared ancestor" down to 2 prime suspects for the role of Spero Armorgie.

PATERNITY SUIT #1: A LOAD OF BULLOCHS?

At the outbreak of hostilities in the Civil War in 1861, the Southern States were in a worse position than the North as the North had the majority of America's manufacturing, arms production and industrial power. The southern states were essentially the primary producers traditionally growing crops of cotton, tobacco, and rice, utilising the labour of slaves as well as indentured servants and landless free persons. Given the South's lack of industrial production, the Confederates were forced to look to Europe. The already strong links from the cotton trade made Liverpool the obvious choice for organising supplies and aid for the Confederacy. It was also important to keep open the supply line for cotton upon which the Lancashire cotton mills depended, and from which the South earned the revenue that funded the Confederate war effort.

That was the geopolitical background that was the lead to my first prime suspect. James Dunwoody Bulloch, a Confederate naval officer, arriving in Liverpool on 4 June 1861 with orders to buy or have constructed 6 steam vessels suitable for use as commerce destroyers against the Union, to be delivered, unarmed, under the British flag at any

Southern port, was not that prime suspect. I just wanted to set the record straight; the record for the longest sentence.

James Dunwoody Bulloch

Much has been written about James Dunwoody Bulloch, and much was written by James Dunwoody Bulloch, however, it was his half-brother, Irvine Stephens Bulloch who became my first prime Spero suspect. Before I move onto describing why Irvine Stephens Bulloch was a person of interest, it is worth understanding the legacy of James Dunwoody Bulloch, not only because I found it fascinating to learn his role in Liverpool's history but he left me a big clue as to who Spero might be.

James Dunwoody Bulloch was described as the European agent of Confederacy and also as a Confederate secret agent, and their "most dangerous man" in Europe, according to Union State Department officials during the

AMERICA'S HOPE

Civil War. It is real cloak and dagger history. He remained in Liverpool after the end of the war and died in 1901. He is buried in Smithdown Road Cemetery, Toxteth, Liverpool, and his gravestone bears the inscription, "An American by birth, an Englishman by choice". James Dunwoody Bulloch was another Confederate exile who took British citizenship.

The clue that James Dunwoody Bulloch left for me was in a letter that I found record of. Part of his role as a Confederate agent was to try to influence British politicians and win support for the Confederates from the wider British population. And who thinks media influence is just a 21st century phenomenon? The letter I found was published in the newspaper the *Liverpool Mercury* on 19 April 1865, 10 days after the end of the American Civil War and Bulloch was already talking up the likelihood of the Confederate States rising again.

The first paragraph of the letter reads:

Gentlemen, as a Southern man, born on Southern soil, but, from circumstances beyond my control, far away, I'm ashamed to say, from the scenes of my countrymen's woes, I am pained that the friends of the South should evince such despondency when in reality the North had achieved at best a barren triumph over her gallant foe.

I include this to show what the loss of the Civil War meant to Bulloch as well as to *evince* the loss of my record as the author of the longest sentence. However, I have just taken the record for the longest build up to extracting the smallest bit of humour. Result.

Bulloch's letter concludes with a Latin motto, *DUM SPIRO SPERO*, which translates as "*While I breathe, I hope*". I am no Latin scholar so had to run it through an online translator, and it turns out Spero is the Latin word for "hope"! This is pretty much in the way that, when put through a text-speak translator, *WTF* comes out as "*I didn't see that coming*".

AMERICA'S HOPE?

In the case of my search, one of the questions "why" is *why* did my great-great-grandfather call himself Spero Armorgie? In the depths of my early cluelessness, I increasingly thought that the answer to this would be not only the most interesting to me but would also be a clue to the "who?" question. The annoying thing is that it took me so long to see the obvious. More annoying is that Shelley led me to the answer and I ignored it. When I say annoying, of course I mean *rewarding*.

This is another digression to allow me to enlarge on my discovery that my great great grandfather's forename meant "Hope" in Latin. Big deal; what about Armorgie? Hope Armorgie? There was no Latin translation I could find for Armorgie – but I will go on to explain how it may have hidden another meaning.

Dum spiro spero, used by James Dunwoody Bulloch, as I have discovered is the state motto of the American state of South Carolina, one of the Confederate states. South Carolina was the first state to secede from the Union and was the founding state in the Confederate States of America.

If I rewind to 29 December 1871, A-Day, the Armorgie genesis, there were 2 documents that gave 2 different spellings of my surname on the records relating to the birth of Reginald Armorgie. On the birth certificate it was spelled **Armorgie** and this is shown as being recorded by Louisa Crossley. On the baptism record the spelling was **Amorgie**, quite possibly spelled by Reg's father who should have been there to prevent raised eyebrows from the vicar. Not raised eyebrows about the strange spelling of **Amorgie**, although I wouldn't blame him, but raised eyebrows if the named father had been absent.

Some people, typically those who are habitual solvers of cryptic crosswords, see every word as an anagram. Shelley put the spelling of Amorgie through her anagram-solver of a brain and spat out the result that **Amorgie** is an anagram of **Amerigo**.

"And?" I asked.

"On 7 August 1501 we dropped our anchor off the shores of that new land, thanking God with solemn prayers and the celebration of the Mass. Once there, we determined that the new land was not an island but a continent..."

This is not my wife's quote, this is a translation of a record written by ***Amerigo Vespucci*** in his letter entitled *Mundus Novus*, sent to Lorenzo di Pierfrancesco de' Medici (1502/1503). Hey, this story goes back well before full market penetration of the Armorgie brand!

In April 1507, this letter was published by *Ringmann* and *Waldseemüller* in their work, *Introduction to Cosmography*, with an accompanying world map. Translated into English, their book included a letter that Vespucci had written, and in a preface to the letter, Ringmann wrote:

"I see no reason why anyone could properly disapprove of a name derived from that of Amerigo, the discoverer, a man of sagacious genius. A suitable form would be Amerige, meaning **Land of Amerigo**, *or* **America**, *since Europe and Asia have received women's names."*

AMERICA'S HOPE

This is apparently the first documented mention of the term "*America*" and, as another fact in an ocean of conjecture, it showed that America was named after *Amerigo Vespucci* (or named "for" *Amerigo Vespucci* as the Americans would say and, hey, it's their country now.) *Amerigo* was one of the several men who supposedly "discovered" America - if, in fact, it had ever been lost and needed discovering. *Amerigo* possibly didn't have the advantage that I had of being able to call upon the help of the medieval ancestor of my friend Gentleman Farmer.

If you are keeping up you will have worked out that **Amerigo** is an anagram of **Amorgie**. Does that make Spero Armorgie/Amorgie a codename for "America's Hope"? While I breathe, I do sincerely hope that is true. And was Spero really "waiting" for the South to rise again as his stated occupation of *waiter* says on his son's birth certificate? Yeah, OK, I'm stretching a point now.

This is why I said earlier that Armorgie is not my real name, or rather *shouldn't* be my name. Maybe it should have been **Amorgie** and not Armorgie. Not that that would stop people from misspelling it. Or maybe it should have been **Amerigo** and those registering the birth and baptism fluffed their lines?

I could hear the words of the ticket seller at Bhowani Junction, "You cannot be Mr Amerigo because that is the name of the man after whom America was named."

Maybe I was lucky to end up as Mr Armorgie.

Finally in Conundrum Corner, I have no knowledge of why the name Reginald was chosen for Louisa and Spero's son. The meaning of Reginald is "King". Do we have *America's Hope* being succeeded by his son, *America's King?* They would have called him Elvis had he been born 85 years later. If you subscribe to the theory of nominative determinism, you will be sadly disappointed by this grand name being given to "King" Reginald who went on to be a convicted pickpocket and *alleged* church roof lead thief.

IN THE TOWN WHERE I WAS BORN LIVED A MAN WHO SAILED TO SEA

Meanwhile, back on the track of finding Spero, James Dunwoody Bulloch had a half-brother, Irvine Stephens Bulloch; they had the same father but different mothers. During the civil War, Irvine was an officer in the Confederate Navy who fired the last shot from *CSS Alabama* before it sank off the coast of Cherbourg, France, in June 1864. I had no idea that American Civil War involved a battle in the English Channel and, interesting rather than suggesting any Armorgie genetic connection, the site of this battle was only about 40 miles from the Island of Sark where one branch of the Armorgie family settled in 1979 and still remain.

After the loss of the *Alabama*, Bulloch dried out and returned to Liverpool from where he was sent out in October 1864 to join the aforementioned *CSS Shenandoah* as sailing master. Irvine navigated the *Shenandoah* from just off San Francisco back to Liverpool, where the captain surrendered on 6 November 1865. Irvine was denied amnesty by the US President and couldn't return to the USA without risking prosecution, so he remained in Liverpool after the war. He worked as a cotton merchant with his brother, James who was also initially denied amnesty.

Irvine Stephens Bulloch

There is a group photograph taken in 1865 of a group of officers from CSS Shenandoah in Leamington Spa that contains Irvine S. Bulloch, as shown in the chapter entitled *Leamington Spa*.

Irvine married on 28 September 1871 in Liverpool, just 2 months before the birth of Reginald Armorgie, and he died at the age of 56 on 14 July 1898 in Colwyn Bay, Wales. He had no children with his wife and the likelihood of progeny from any other relationship is unproven[14].

Remember Theodore "Teddy" Roosevelt's diary entry of 27 May, 1869, where he wrote, "went to our cousin's school at Waterloo"? The Bulloch brothers were the uncles of Theodore Roosevelt, and James Bulloch was living in Waterloo at the time the Roosevelts visited. One of Irvine's

---

[14] *nota bene*, as the lawyers say in Washington DC.

sisters was **Martha "Mittie" Stewart Bulloch** and she married Theodore Roosevelt Sr. Mittie was therefore the mother of US President Theodore Roosevelt (Jr.) and also the paternal grandmother of Anna Eleanor Roosevelt, wife of US President Franklin Delano Roosevelt.

I mentioned previously about how William Long's and Louisa Crossley's marriage certificate contained the information that held the key to me finding my metaphorical way to Bath. One of the witnesses at that ceremony, and who signed the certificate, was named **Martha Stewart**. The name, I am sure, is coincidental[15], although interestingly Martha Stewart Bulloch Roosevelt was not in the USA on 8 January 1873 at the time of William and Louisa's wedding, as she and her family were on a European Grand Tour, arriving back in the USA later on 5 November 1873.

I couldn't find a record of exactly where Martha Roosevelt was on the date of that wedding but Teddy Roosevelt's diaries show that he, his father and his brother were on what looked like an all-male side trip in Egypt and Palestine. Despite my searching, I am not sure where Martha was on that date.

I have looked at the signature of Martha Stewart (upper) on the marriage certificate of William and Louisa and have compared it to a signature on a letter written by Martha "Mittie" Stewart Bulloch (lower).

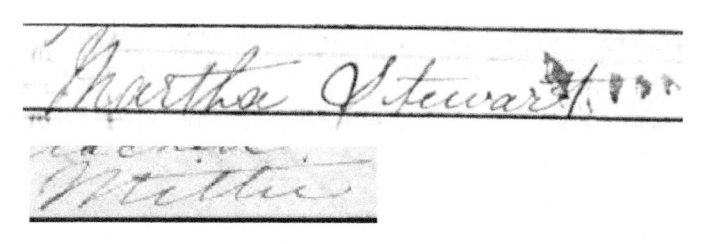

---

[15] *nota bene*, as the lawyers say in Washington DC.

I am no graphologist but neither of those signatures looks like Times New Roman font. Any conclusion is yours to make.

At the time of me fishing around to find some connection to Irvine Stephens Bulloch so that I could really pimp up my family tree, my DNA evidence came to the Roosevelts' rescue. I found out that it really was apparently a load of Bullochs. I was grateful for the assistance of Robert Naylor[16] in Washington DC, a man who shares my passion for ancestry investigation and who is a proven, direct descendant from the Bulloch ancestors. My DNA analysis results were compared to Robert's but there was no identified match which I would have expected had I been descended from Irvine Stephens Bulloch. In God (and DNA) we trust.

---

[16] *nota bene*, not a lawyer in Washington DC.

PATERNITY SUIT #2: SKIP TO MY LOU(ISA)

With Irvine Stephens Bulloch it was the DNA evidence that did not support any suggestion that he was Spero Armorgie. With my second prime suspect the connection *was* supported by DNA evidence but other documents disproved the connection. Francis Thornton Chew was a Confederate naval officer who had been on the previously mentioned *CSS Shenandoah*, so I knew had been in Liverpool, at least in November 1865. Tick.

On investigation I found that Francis Thornton Chew had a Scottish great grandfather on his mother's side. Tick.

I had 3 living people to whom I was DNA matched who shared one of his maternal great great grandfathers. Tick.

I had 17 living people to whom I was DNA matched who descended directly from a common Chew ancestor, 15 of whom are descended from the first Chew settler in the USA, John Chew. Francis Thornton Chew is descended from John Chew. Tick.

John Chew was born on 16 July 1587 in Lancashire, England and sailed to America in 1622, so to be fair, this distant date would diminish the likelihood of proving a triangulated DNA connection that would show any connection that would link me to Francis Thornton Chew.

COLIN ARMORGIE

Francis Thornton Chew

The documentary evidence I tracked down that clinched that Francis Thornton Chew wasn't in Liverpool in 1871 was an entry in the St. Louis, Missouri, City Directory of 1871, which showed his address and his occupation as freight agent. From an officer in the Confederate States Navy who circumnavigated the globe to becoming a freight agent... such are the fortunes of war. There were other records, including his marriage there in 1872, the births of his children, census entries and his death there in 1894.

I suppose Louisa could have gone to St. Louis, got pregnant and returned to England, but I suspect not and I couldn't find any records on passenger lists, immigration records, etc. For those who doubted my conjecture about Francis Thornton Chew, please have a look out of the window to see if it really is raining.

Finally, take a bonus point for having identified that the song "*Skip to my Lou*(isa)" is a song from the musical *Meet me in St. Louis*. Don't make me explain any more.

CAUGHT UP IN THE DOUBLE HELIX

You may rightly be questioning how I can have identified DNA matches to 20 different, living people who apparently share DNA with Francis Thornton Chew if I don't share DNA with him. The thing is, that's not necessarily true though. There is no evidence to say that I *don't* share DNA with Francis Thornton Chew, but *absence of evidence* is no use when trying to prove something. Unless you are Reg Armorgie who was caught apparently going equipped to nick lead off a church roof.

Yes, I quite possibly *do* share DNA with Francis Thornton Chew but that doesn't mean he is the father of Reginald Armorgie. I can't prove it definitively as I haven't found any DNA connection to any living *descendant* of Francis Thornton Chew. All the connections I found were to his forebears. If I were to find a DNA match to a proven descendant, that would be so much more significant.

To give some perspective in terms of DNA being a numbers game, let's look back at John Chew, who I identified as the common ancestor and triangulated source for 15 of my DNA matches. If John Chew had 4 children and each of those had 4 children, and so on, for, say, 12 generations to bring us up to today, that would amount to him potentially having about 17million descendants alive today; give or take a couple.

I had staked too much reliance on DNA evidence and I needed to reel back to look more holistically at all the evidence - or absence of it, your honour. This knocked me back and left me wondering how I would ever get any closer to certainty or, indeed, *if* I would get any closer to certainty. On reflection, I decided that I needed more reliable evidence, a modicum of conjecture to replace any missing pieces and scrutiny by others. I carried on.

According to genealogical expertise, however, any DNA matches that I have would be connected to me in the last 5 generations if going directly back. Any further back and the levels of shared segments of DNA would be too small to reliably detect. If the DNA connection had "sideways" elements through cousins, then from our shared ancestor the generational distance would be less than 5 generations.

I was seeking my great great grandfather, 4 generations back, so I would be in the range of being able to reasonably accurately detect a connection to a DNA connection. The biggest challenge I had, was actually finding a *descendant* of someone who had taken a DNA test and loaded the results to one of the websites where mine were loaded. Was I feeling lucky? No less a lucky feeling than buying a National Lottery ticket.

There was a chance. Playing the numbers game again, I reckoned that any great great grandparent could be expected to have about 1,000 living descendants based on the average of 4 children per generation. The odds of me getting lucky had gone up a little but probably only to needle-in-a-haystack levels.

I have subsequently found where Francis Thornton Chew's family lineage overlaps with and shares the lineage of the man I will go on to identify as Spero Armorgie. The background to this surprised me but was in the realms of being explicable. Again, it comes down to a numbers game,

AMERICA'S HOPE

and anyone who glazes over at the sight of more numbers will already have skipped out of this chapter so I can quite easily call them foolish without actually upsetting them.

Today the population of the USA is about 340 million. In 1870 it was about 39m, only 11% of what it is today, but still a significant number. In researching my DNA matches with ancestry in those eastern seaboard states, I found it was quite a closed community. The early settlers had acquired tracts of land and there was inter-marriage amongst those families. The same surnames persisted with relatively little dilution, certainly up until the Civil War.

EVIDENCE FROM THE HISTORY OF AMERICAN SETTLEMENT

In 18th century North America there was a significant wave of immigrants who settled the southern colonies. The settlers were typically farmers from the northern England borders, from the southernmost counties of Scotland, and from Ulster, fleeing hard times and religious persecution. Between 250,000 and 400,000 Scots-Irish people migrated to America in the 18th century, and that ethnic group soon became the dominant one in the interior of the southern states and in the Appalachian region from Pennsylvania to Georgia. These Scots-Irish immigrants mingled in communities with second generation and later English settlers.

I am looking for the potential links that my family has with people, one person in fact, Spero, who may have come from this pool of American immigrants, however, I don't lose sight of the significance of the parallel involuntary immigration into this area of African slaves. Between 1700 and 1740, a large majority of the net overseas migration to the southern colonies were Africans. In fact, I have noted that I have DNA matches to African Americans still living in this area today. In the third quarter of the 18th century, the population of this region amounted to roughly 55% British, 38% black, and 7% German.

In later times, between 1880 and 1920, there was rapid industrialisation and urbanisation accompanied by America receiving more than 20 million immigrants, with those immigrants coming more widely from Central, Eastern and Southern Europe. This wave of immigration was more associated with the north eastern states of the USA and not so much to the southern states, whose economies remained largely based on agriculture.

This brief analysis of the settlement of America in a short period could make me look guilty of fitting an explanation to my DNA analysis, looking for justification of southern states American-Scottish ancestry in my paternal line – an ancestry that I had no documented evidence to support. This may be so but I wanted to understand if American-Scottish ancestry were at least a possibility, and then I would seek other evidence to support or disprove it.

BREAKTHROUGH!

We live in a world where the future is unpredictable but the big surprise comes when the past is also found to be unpredictable.

When I received the results of my DNA test, I noticed that I had many DNA matches to Americans who had taken tests. This was perhaps unsurprising given the higher interest amongst Americans in ancestry research and so many American's having UK ancestry. About the same time I took my test my wife also took a DNA test and the comparison of our experiences was interesting. No, we didn't find we were related (other than by marriage) but her results showed far fewer connections to Americans than mine. Maybe I could expect to find Spero amongst the suspected American connection, but maybe it's the same expectation as expecting to win the jackpot in the National Lottery just because I've bought a ticket. It was more hope than expectation but if you believe in nominative determinism, then Spero "Hope" Armorgie would be watching over me.

I was narrowing my research down to identifying those of my DNA matches who had family trees that included any of the people from my Liverpool Americans list. Over a year later I found the answer - eureka! The answer was that

I **couldn't** find a plausible connection; that is one borne out by DNA evidence and all those other things in my strategy that I previously explained, **excluding** trusting to a silver dollar, or a rabbit's foot on a string, or a four leaf clover, or even an old horse shoe, uh-huh huh. Thunkyoovurmush.

At some points in my investigation I was maybe losing the plot but I haven't seen any evidence to suggest I that wasn't taking it as seriously as I should. My use of the vacuum cleaner on my lawn was just a tactic to ensure that the neighbours didn't interrupt my research, and telling the kids I'd moved to America kept them away for a while.

I had been looking west across the Atlantic Ocean for the best part of two years when the best lead I found to my most convincing putative link to Spero was from a woman who lives in the London Borough of Croydon, England, just 135 miles *east* of where I now live. I went to school 12 miles from Croydon. The crazy, amazing thing about family tree research is that the obvious is never seen until it finds you. It could be argued that what I found wasn't obvious; it was just that I was looking in the wrong place. Isn't that the same thing, really? This was the piece of luck I couldn't legislate for in my strategy to find Spero, as he hadn't come up in the rigour of all my other investigations to date.

"*Lady Luck smiles on those who continue their efforts*" is a quote by American investor and financial commentator, Jim Rogers. I quite like it because I think the other end of my rainbow being found in Croydon was the luck I was rewarded with for diligence and perseverance in my search. The other lesson I got from Jim was that if you devote too much effort on one thing to the exclusion of others, it can have another consequence; in Jim's case, he made a lot of money but he's on his 3rd marriage.

Georgiana Walker was Louisa Crossley's employer in Liverpool and I had acquired a copy of Georgiana's diary. After I had drawn a blank researching possible connections to the visitors she mentioned to her homes in Liverpool and Leamington Spa, I looked at other connections she had had in her time in Halifax Nova Scotia and in Bermuda during the Civil War. I was hungry for information on her experience of the American Civil War as it was so personal and so different to all the academic works on that period in history.

Georgiana's diary entry of 19 March 1865, in the last months of the Civil War, living in Bermuda, states:

"*Although communication with the coast has been cut off, we still see many of our countrymen; & it is a great pleasure to me, to be able to welcome them to our home. Capt Maffitt, Capt Lowe, Col Andrews, Captain Davidson, Mr Howell, Mr Carter, our good friend, and many others have been here of late.*"

Captain Maffitt and Mr Carter were already known to me, being on my Liverpool American list but were known to not have valid Spero credentials. The editor of my copy of the diary had annotated it to describe that Mr Howell was Jefferson Davis's brother-in-law. I determined who Col. Andrews was, and Capt. Lowe, and was able to exclude them from the list of Spero suspects. Captain Davidson, however, was a different consideration; the diary editor had more to say about Captain Davidson:

"*Hunter Davidson of the District of Columbia served aboard the* Patrick Henry, *in 1861, the* Virginia (Merrimack) *in 1862, and abroad in 1864; and in 1864-1965 he commanded the* City of Richmond."

He was a blockade runner and was abroad in 1864, presumably not just in Bermuda. As with the others, it was easy to find information on Hunter Davidson. Don't believe me? Google his name. Amongst other things he has a Wikipedia page but it said nothing about him having been in Liverpool. It was worth investigation and I was like a Hound Dog with a bone, and can reveal that there was absolutely no truth to the rumour that I ain't never caught a rabbit. I was now a Hunter hunter. See what I did there?

"Elvis, join the queue over there with Mrs Davies and Gentleman Farmer; your work in my story is done, thunkyoovurmush."

Hunter Davidson

Before I undertook the more arduous search for evidence, I thought it would be worth me checking for any potential DNA match I had to anyone with Hunter Davidson in their family tree. That sounds like a big job performing a DNA / family tree search but, actually, the search facilities on ancestry websites make it relatively quick and simple. It's from that search where I found a reasonably strong DNA match to Nicola Gowan. Was she a

AMERICA'S HOPE

resident of the Southern States? Yes, a resident of the south London state of Croydon.

Nicola's family tree showed that she was the great great granddaughter of Hunter Davidson. Her relationship was documented and so my question was whether I could find any evidence that I might be Hunter Davidson's great great grandson?

"*I trust to history for the answer.*" This is a quote from an open letter in May 1874 written by Hunter Davidson himself.

RESPICE FINEM

*"I remember that a distinguished Admiral sent word to me when under a flag of truce during the war, that if I came down to his squadron again in a certain boat, he would not respect the flag, as he did not acknowledge that I was engaged in civilized or legitimate warfare. This glanced from my armor as many a worse shot did from my **own** side, though for other reasons, for I felt that as he was the only sufferer then, he saw the matter from but one point of view, but that time would set it even as I replied in substance to the officer,* **respice finem.**"

This is a further quote from the same 1874 rambling letter by Hunter Davidson and says a lot about the man. Davidson was bitter about the treatment he received from his Confederate ex-comrades in the time after the Civil War, he was also responding to the criticism from his former enemies that he "fought dirty", and it showed he had a grasp of Latin. I'll give you the clues, you make the connections.

Respice finem means to have regard for the end or to consider the outcome. I might adopt that as the motto for my investigations into Spero's identity. Or is it a veiled warning?

COLIN ARMORGIE

I thought that Reginald Armorgie lived an eventful life but the more I found about Hunter Davidson, the more I was amazed that it was a life lived less ordinary. At the outset I had an initial doubt about Davidson's credentials to be a Spero candidate, particularly when I saw that he was born in 1826. Louisa Crossley was born in 1845 and was therefore nearly 20 years his junior. I quickly discovered other information that Hunter Davidson, if he actually were Spero, could have been behaving, shall we say, "in character". This part of his character will later become apparent.

Hunter Davidson is also referred to as J Hunter Davidson. I haven't found any reference to the name that the J might be an initial for. He had 2 brothers Roger **Jones** Davidson and **John** Wynn "Black Jack" Davidson. My brother, Paul, has carried on the family tradition by marrying a Jane and giving his 3 children forenames all beginning with J. This works quite well until your hearing starts to fail in later years. Sorry, Paul, I SAID THAT THIS WORKS QUITE WELL UNTIL YOUR HEARING STARTS TO FAIL IN LATER YEARS.

Hunter Davidson was the son of a US Army officer and a mother with a long Virginian lineage; Hunter was his mother's maiden surname. His great grandfather was John Hunter, born in 1721 in Hunterston, Ayrshire, Scotland, and immigrated to America. I'll give you the clues, you make the connections.

Hunter's father was William Baker (possibly Benjamin?) Davidson II, who was born 1795 in Virginia and died of disease in Florida in the Seminole Wars in 1840. Hunter's 3x great grandfather was John James Davidson, born in 1675 in Legacorry (og an Choire), County Armagh, Ulster, and immigrated to America. After the death of his father, Hunter was found a position as an acting midshipman in the US Navy. Which way to Liverpool?

In 1852 Hunter Davidson married Mary Steele Ray in Maryland, USA, with whom he had 6 children between 1854 and 1872. When I look at his life in this period, he spent much of it away from his home, so Mary must have come to realise the consequence of being notified that Hunter had shore leave. His children were born in places as diverse as Maryland, Virginia and North Carolina, possibly as a consequence of the ebb and flow of the war rather than the ebb and flow of the tide.

Hunter Davidson had a 20 year career serving primarily in the Pacific during the Mexican War, in the Coast Survey, and in the African Squadron helping to suppress the international slave trade. He was one of a handful of officers selected to return the British Arctic exploration vessel, *HMS Resolute*, to the UK in 1856. He wasn't just a time-served seafarer; he established his skills as an inventor and received two patents for a lifeboat-lifting device. In April 1861, the US government paid him $10,000 for the device, worth about $342,000 in 2023 terms. It was probably a fluke of timing rather than a show of ingratitude, but by the end of that month, Hunter resigned his commission and transferred his services to the Virginia State Navy. By the end of 1861, the Virginia State Navy was absorbed by the Confederate States Navy.

MANO A MANO

As if war of any sort isn't a terrible thing, a civil war is arguably even worse, with a country split in two by disagreements so strong that countrymen will take arms against countrymen. In the case of the Davidson family the symbolism of a divided nation was horribly manifested by a divided family; whilst Hunter sided with the Confederates, his brother, John Wynn Davidson sided with the Union. John Wynn became a brigadier general in the United States Army. After the war, he commanded the 10th Cavalry, known as the *Buffalo Soldiers*. It was there that he acquired the nickname "Black Jack", as his regiment was a segregated African American unit.

In the Confederate States Navy, Davidson commanded a number of different ships in combat and as blockade runners, but in May 1862 he became shore-based and started to assist Commander Matthew Fontaine Maury, in establishing a barrier of electrical "torpedoes" on the James River, Virginia. Not that it really matters in the context of this story but these torpedoes were perhaps more recognisable as submarine mines rather than self-propelling underwater missiles.

The quote from Hunter Davidson at the start of a previous chapter was effectively a long missive about his perceived sleight at not having received what he considered to be proper recognition for his role in development of mine warfare. He was also defending accusations that the use of hidden, underwater mines was somehow against the unwritten, almost chivalrous rules of combat, where a fair fight required combatants to virtually look each other in the eye.

Maury left Davidson in charge of the Submarine Battery Service when he left to travel to England, and in the summer of 1862 through to July 1864, Davidson developed the Submarine Battery Service into a formidable system of not only defence but also attack. On 9 April 1864, he took the small torpedo boat *Squib* down the James River on a daring mission to Newport News, where he attacked the US Navy frigate *Minnesota* with a spar torpedo and was able to escape back up the James. A spar torpedo was effectively an explosive device on the end of a long pole extending from the bow of a ship. In recognition of this feat, Hunter Davidson was promoted to the rank of Commander, although the biggest reward was possibly that he didn't get killed.

Later in 1864 Davidson travelled to England to assist Maury with acquiring more torpedo materials and running them through the blockade back to a Confederate port. This was 1864 and Reginald Armorgie was not born until 1871; yes, it could have been a long gestation but let's go with 9 months as the more usual length. With this apparent absence from the UK between 1864 and 1871, how did Hunter Davidson fall under my suspicion? The answer is that it turned out to not be his last visit across the Atlantic, as I will go on to explain.

Davidson's next Civil War service was as Commanding Officer of the blockade runner *City of Richmond*, which he sailed from London in December 1864 to Cherbourg, France, where he transferred to *CSS Stonewall* , the ship in which he probably arrived in Bermuda when he was mentioned in Georgiana Walker's diary on 19 March 1865. Following that, during the final days of the Confederacy, Davidson found himself in command of the Confederate torpedo defences of Galveston, Texas.

He got around a bit – which is different to putting it around a bit.

MAVERICK AND ICEMAN

As if Hunter Davidson had not done enough to be moving towards becoming a bitter old legend and inventor, here's something he probably didn't realise the significance of; Hunter Davidson was the captain of the world's first aircraft carrier. How so – the first manned flight was not until 1903?

At this point I am contractually bound, by the contract of marriage, to fly Saint Piran's flag for the people of Cornwall. Like Spero's story, there is an unofficial and unrecorded claim that the first successful sustained powered aeroplane flight was made by Richard Pearse, a Cornish farmer in April 1903, 8 months before Orville and Wilbur Wright secured their place in history in December 1903.

This is a tenuous link, or no link at all, to events on 1 July 1862 on the James River in Virginia. Hunter Davidson was ordered to take *CSS Teaser* on a special mission to carry and launch a coal-gas filled, silk observation balloon to reconnoitre the Union Army's positions along the James River. To accomplish this *CSS Teaser* carried the balloon tethered to its deck from where it could be reeled up to the observation altitude. From the basket under the balloon as the ship sailed up the river, Confederate observers were to log the positions of the Union Army.

COLIN ARMORGIE

Any success from this pioneering flight from the world's first aircraft carrier was short-lived. Soon after this successful balloon reconnaissance mission, the Union Navy sent ships to counter *CSS Teaser* and other Confederate vessels in the James River. At dawn on 4 July 1862, *CSS Teaser* was preparing a second balloon flight to map Union positions when the Union ships arrived. A fierce gun battle ensued and when *CSS Teaser* was disabled, the crew were ordered to abandon ship and swim to safety. At least I learned that Hunter Davidson could swim even though I have yet to find his certificate for 25 yards breaststroke.

In another strange quirk of genealogical fate, this time involving Wales rather than Cornwall, I discovered one more intrepid relative of mine was a pioneer hero of balloon flight. My father's maternal uncle, Rowland William Griffiths was in the Royal Flying Corps in WWI and died in an observation balloon flight over the desert near Basra, Iraq in November 1917. One could have assumed that he was shot down but I had to search for the truth (hey, that's my *modus operandi*) and the truth was less dramatic; the balloon was rapidly deflated by a squally gust of wind that resulted in it plunging fatally to the desert floor.

This possibly explains why I have an irrational fear of heights – but doesn't fully explain why I can misuse and overuse Latin phrases.

THE SLEEP OF SWORDS

You will remember the fate of other former Confederate States Navy officers in the period after the end of the Civil War, ending up in civilian jobs, a far cry from the lives they lived during the conflict. Of course, life turned out differently for Hunter Davidson when the war ended; he was an unemployed 39 year old father of four young children and the only career he had ever known came to an end. Hunter Davidson knew the sea, and in common with some other ex-Confederate naval officers in the same position, he hoped to obtain work in commercial shipping or with a foreign navy.

I found a record of Hunter's preparation for this civilian life; on 8 August 1865, 4 months after the end of the Civil War, he was in London acquiring his Master's Certificate from the UK Board of Trade. I don't know why he chose to take this qualification in the UK rather than the USA but he was turning out to be the transatlantic frequent flyer of his day.

In late 1865, Hunter Davidson landed a job that he referred to as a "torpedo expedition" and his wife described as "a fine position in the Chilean Navy with a good salary & the prospect of making money." A rarity in my family history, a male ancestor appeared to make the better prediction than his wife. It did not turn out to be a fine position with the opportunity of making money. As I have seen in the writing of several ex-Confederates, Davidson styled himself as the "hard up Confederate" as he spent more than two years searching not only for another job, but also for a home.

A job in Liverpool would be too convenient to my story, wouldn't it? Life rarely serves up such opportunity on a plate so I had to hunt for my clues.

POACHER TURNED GAMEKEEPER

As much as Davidson possibly didn't want to be part of the new United States of America establishment and was precluded from taking a role in their military, I suspect more out of necessity in 1868 he took the position of commander of Maryland Oyster Police. The word "what?" immediately comes to mind. I am happy if I can make every day a school day, so I will explain that this organisation had more gravitas and significance than the Cornish Sardine Cops[17].

The background to this diversion of mine was that in the early 19th century there was depletion of oysters from over-fishing in the waters on the US eastern seaboard, sometimes referred to as the Oyster Wars. The depletion of oysters was initially worse in New England and the oystermen from there started coming south into the waters of Maryland and Virginia. Legislation to control fishing in in Virginian waters resulted in more dredgers coming into Maryland waters and the livelihoods of local oystermen were threatened.

Legislation was passed in Maryland to regulate who, how and when oysters could be taken, but the new laws

---

[17] Standard uxorial contractual obligations apply

were hard to enforce since lawbreakers generally outnumbered the authorities, combined with there being a large tract of open water to control. The Maryland Oyster Police can be seen as an early sort of environmental enforcement agency in Chesapeake Bay, originally staffed by the county sheriffs, and results were consequentially of limited effectiveness. Enter The Enforcer: Hunter Davidson, no stranger to conflict resolution.

The steamer *Leila* was built in Baltimore in 1869 as the flagship of this single state "navy". It was named after Hunter Davidson's first child, his daughter Leila, a player of note in Spero's story. Davidson mounted a big fuck-off 12 pounder gun on the deck and set about his appointed business. He set about his business with a no-messing approach that I'd like to think I have inherited, and prepared the initial "Internal Rules and Regulations" and "Shipping Articles," which each officer and crewman had to sign when joining the navy. I think a lot of things; Hunter Davidson was more a man of action.

Inevitably, Davidson got frustrated with the lack of support he was getting from certain members of the Maryland judiciary, and he didn't hold back in voicing it:

"Nearly all of these cases have first to go before the Justices of the Peace, whose total want of education, in some instances, renders them unable to comprehend a case, or pronounce an intelligent judgment."

We've all worked with people like that, and given Davidson's background, his skills were not of the political kind; in military terms he would be described as "mission-oriented" and his effectiveness was probably more to do with the no-nonsense reputation he developed than the back-up of the legislature. I would have liked to have him in my corner to front up to Mrs Davies at parents' evening.

His frustration inevitably got the better of him and he started looking for other employment opportunities. Hunter

AMERICA'S HOPE

Davidson left the service in 1872 and has become something of a local legend in Maryland. The Maryland Oyster Police still exists today as the Maryland Natural Resources Police and Davidson's legacy still endures as this image of a modern day Maryland T-shirt shows. I wear mine to tell a story, regardless of "if". It is a visual aid to answer the age-old question of "where does your name come from?"

NOT A LOT OF PEOPLE KNOW THIS

Whilst still nominally in the employ of the Maryland Oyster Police, Hunter Davidson was contacted by the US President, Ulysses S. Grant, about a special mission on behalf of the American government. I found a written piece by John Mercer Brooke, 1826-1906, in which he describes how the President sent Davidson as a defence contractor to make approaches to the German states in the Franco-Prussian War. As a side note, Brooke was part of the Confederate old-boys network, the designer of the *CSS Virginia*, inventor of the Brooke Rifle, and chief of the Confederacy's naval ordnance bureau.

Davidson's presidential role was not as a political envoy, understandably given Davidson's demonstrated 'abilities' in this respect, but very much in respect of looking to sell American manufactured arms, ammunition and ships to the Prussians. Brooke described it as a "failed trip" but, crucially, I take a different stance.

In the same way that I had no idea about the dates of the American Civil War, I had a similar blank space where information should be on the Franco-Prussian War. Along with so many other trails I investigated that came to nothing, I investigated this one. The Franco-Prussian War ended on 10 May 1871.

COLIN ARMORGIE

In another place in the world on 28 January 1871, Chesapeake Bay, Maryland, USA, the Maryland Oyster Police vessel, *Leila*, was boarded by pirates. The captain, Hunter Davidson, was asleep in his cabin when he heard a commotion outside his door. In true Hunter Davidson act-now-ask-questions-later style, the captain took his revolver and fired two shots through the panelling on his door. I reckon he shot from the hip – in more ways than one. The pirates fled in the face of this opposition, shortly to be captured and detained in the parallel Davidson no-fucking-messing style.

Apart from being another good story painting a picture of the sort of man that Davidson was, the date was important. It was after this date that Davidson departed for Europe on his special mission. This was the end of January 1871 and I reckon Reginald Armorgie must have been conceived about the end of March 1871. You know where this going, metaphorically and geographically... look out, Liverpool!

CONJECTURE WARNING!

Hunter Davidson would likely have crossed the Atlantic into the principal transatlantic port of Liverpool, where he could have received a friendly welcome from and renewed acquaintances with ex-Confederate colleagues; possibly the Bullochs, possibly the Walkers. Did he perhaps stay at or maybe have been entertained at 19 Abercromby Square, or maybe have gone via ex-Confederate acquaintances in Leamington Spa on his way to London to join a ship crossing the channel to continental Europe?

Davidson would very likely have been on the European side of the Atlantic for a period sometime between 28 January 1871 and 10 May 1871. Reports of the history of the conflict tell of the neutrality of Belgium and, given its position between the territories of the warring sides,

AMERICA'S HOPE

America's desire to remain neutral, it is quite conceivable that Hunter Davidson went to meet Prussian representatives on neutral territory.

Was Belgium where Davidson went to meet the Prussians? If so, would be have gone to the principal port of Antwerp? I only ask because when, in 1884, the young errand boy, Reginald Armorgie, was convicted of theft, he gave his place of birth as Antwerp. How would the name of Antwerp even be known to a young boy in the north of England? I wonder if Reg had, perhaps, been told in some discussion his mother that his real father was from Antwerp / been in Antwerp / had some connection to a gooseberry bush in Antwerp? It is just strange that Reg thought he had been born in Antwerp and not Bath.

Furthermore, there is unusually no evidence of Louisa Crossley's whereabouts in the 1871 census of England and Wales. Was she perhaps out of the country accompanying Hunter Davidson abroad on the date of the census on 2 April 1871? I appreciate that there are many questions, however, if Spero's life story is one big mystery, the events and whereabouts of the key players in this crucial period *still* remains a mystery.

As for the classification of this as a "failed trip" for Davidson, it could be argued, by me, if the trip had failed, then I possibly wouldn't be here to tell this story. Not that I am biased or anything.

Conjecture is all I have for this aspect of Davidson's life but I have hopefully painted a picture of a quite conceivable set of events and places. See what I did there with my choice of words? I'll give you the clues, by auto-suggestion if necessary, and you make the connections.

HAS ANYONE SEEN SPERO?

I wanted to consider as much evidence as I could gather, combined with supposition to fill the gaps, so the obvious question for me was, "Who was the man called Spero 'Amorgie' who stood with Louisa Crossley by the font in St Saviour's church in Bath on 29 December 1871 for Reginald Amorgie's baptism?" Was it Hunter Davidson?

The answer, disappointingly, is that I don't know for definite. I *do* have evidence that Hunter Davidson was in Europe in *early* 1871 when he was attempting to visit the Prussian military, but when did he return to the USA or, indeed, disappear somewhere else in the world? The best evidence I have for this is that Hunter's and his wife, Mary's, last child, Maury Davidson, was born on 7 July 1872. By deduction, this places Hunter in the USA in November 1871, probably in Maryland. So I can conclude that he had left the UK in 1871 *before* Reg's baptism and birth registration.

It would be in the dramatic script if he *had* remained in the UK to "do the decent" thing by Louisa, always allowing for him actually being Reg's father. I have already covered the fact that he was a married man, and nearly 20 years Louisa's senior, and that this was Victorian England, so he may not even have known about Louisa's condition. It therefore remains unknown who was posing as Spero on that day but whoever it was, it wasn't anyone that Louisa was married to.

THINGS START TO GO SOUTH FROM HERE

Hunter "Spero" Davidson had officially served with the Maryland Oyster Police until February 1872, despite his service having been interrupted in 1871 by his presidentially requested side-trip to woo the Prussian military. In about March or April 1872 in New York, Davidson met with Commodore Thomas J. Page, a former Confederate naval officer who was now in service with the Argentine Navy. Davidson was likely looking for his next employment opportunity and Page referred him to Dr Manuel Garcia, the Argentine Minister in London.

In about June 1872, Davidson did meet with Garcia in Paris, possibly London, where he secured his next employment. Hunter Davidson was hired to head the Argentine Navy Torpedo and Hydrographic Bureau. Since returning to the USA after seeing Garcia, Davidson tried to recruit other ex-Confederate experts to accompany him. Also whilst in New York preparing to depart for Argentina, he published a short pamphlet. "*The First Successful Application of Electrical Torpedoes or Submarine Mines in Time of War, and As a System of Defense*". It wasn't the snappy sort of title, like "*America's Hope*", that would have made it an instant best-seller and it was really more of a CV or an egotistical puff piece as it incorporated the testimonials Davidson had solicited from ex-Confederate colleagues after the war.

In this pamphlet he made the bold claim that, "*The results [of Davidson's torpedo system] were that the first vessels ever injured or destroyed in war, by electrical torpedoes, were by the torpedo department operating under my immediate command, and I may add, the only ones that I am aware of.*" I can imagine that getting trumpet players was perhaps difficult and so Davidson, ever resourceful, had to blow his own trumpet. Probably a trumpet he designed himself as well; I don't know.

This was just another example of Davidson's determination to defend his professional reputation. In another such public exchange he had a pop at Jefferson Davis, ex-president of the Confederate States. Davis had given all the credit for the Confederacy's torpedo work to his friend, Brigadier General Gabriel J. Rains, and did not even mention Davidson or the Submarine Battery Service in his book, "*The Rise and Fall of the Confederate Government*" (1881). Davidson put down his trumpet and loaded his guns. He wrote Davis an indignant letter, and Davis replied in a manner that Davidson regarded as "an aggravated repetition of the injustice you have done me in your book". Tell it like it is, Hunter! Davidson pledged to "use whatever means I am possessed to give them all possible publicity." He later published the exchange in several widely read periodicals and kept up his attacks on Davis for decades. As if it wasn't bad enough for Davis being defeated in the Civil War, having Davidson chewing for years at what was left of his reputation wouldn't have been his preferred bedtime reading.

HOW MUCH FURTHER SOUTH IS THIS GOING?

Davidson's feud with Davis could be interpreted as that of an egotist who was determined to defend his place in history, as so many former Civil War officers did in the pages of popular magazines after the war. Hunter Davidson was perhaps proud of his achievements and was probably more trying to defend his credibility as a pioneer in naval technology and thus promote his hoped for personal livelihood.

Hunter Davidson eventually moved to Argentina; the exact date is uncertain as he was something of a commuter between Buenos Aires, New York and England. This move to Argentina, and him choosing to remain in South America after his retirement, ironically all but assured his own obscurity. He hadn't lost his ego as there is still evidence of letters he wrote while he was in South America that were published in newspapers and magazines in the USA, however, he was out of sight and largely out of mind - until I managed to rediscover him for my purposes in my research. I wasn't necessarily looking for the services of a naval torpedo expert but I was looking for a legacy; and I found it. Whether it is part of Armorgie legacy is another question.

Historians who have reviewed Davidson's claim to historical fame have likened his life to one of many similar, forgotten Confederate naval officers whose innovations and zeal made it possible for the Confederacy to challenge and hold out for so long against the numerically superior US Union Navy. This is recognition of a sort but historians' judgements focus largely on those who are no longer around to read them.

ME LLAMO HUNTER DAVIDSON

Hunter Davidson could have been back in England in late 1872, a year after Reg's birth. I found a record of Hunter Davidson departing Liverpool, again, on board the ship *Java*, and arriving in New York on 1 January 1873. I suspect this visit was with Dr Manuel Garcia, the Argentinian who hired him, to advise on the building of ships for the Argentine Navy. Interestingly, in one of his letters to Argentine President Sarmiento, dated 23 April 1874, Dr Garcia warned that "Davidson must be kept on a short leash."

Davidson arrived in Buenos Aires later in 1873 and began to establish a floating torpedo (submarine mines) defence system. In late 1874 Davidson was appointed commanding officer of the Argentine Torpedo Division on the Luján River. Reports tell us that the depot ship blew up in an unfortunate explosion in 1877 but that Davidson was exonerated from any blame. I think Reginald Armorgie may have inherited those sloping shoulders.

Davidson subsequently appears to have been found a position where he could do less damage; in September 1875 he oversaw the laying of a submarine communication cable linking Buenos Aires to the torpedo station on the island of Martín García. Latterly he undertook exploration of the rivers that went into the interior of the South American continent, looking at navigability and assessing the riverside lands for colonisation.

I found no evidence of Hunter Davidson's (first) wife or family ever having joined him in South America but I have found various pieces that show Hunter made various visits away from his time there. There is a renewal of his Master's Certificate with the UK Board of Trade in London on 22 January 1875, and I have found a portrait photograph taken in a London studio in 1875.

He had a liking for London photographic studios; I found another portrait taken in London on 10 March 1880. If it had been today he would have left an endorsement on Reevoo. It was a long way to come just for a photograph, so he was quite possibly visiting his daughter, Leila, who was living in London at that time. This connection is covered in the section *The Gowan connection*.

Davidson also appears on the 1880 US census, probably on that same trip away from South America when he visited London. He was on the same census return as his wife, Mary, with the other 5 of his children, aged between 22 and 7; his children would hardly have known their father given his time spent away from the USA. The family were living in Cambridge, Dorchester, Maryland, and his occupation was given as "agent", whatever that is.

Hunter resigned from the Argentinian naval service in September 1885, and moved to Paraguay for "a retired and quiet life". I found a newspaper story published in The Saint Paul Globe, Minnesota, in 1899 which mentions various Americans who were living in Villa Rica, Paraguay; one of them was identified as "Capt. Hunter Davidson, an unreconstructed Southerner, who left the United States at the close of the Civil War and finally got to Paraguay." He was reported to be running a cattle ranch. Hey, if Errol Flynn could play a pirate and a cowboy then so could J Hunter Davidson!

In a similar newspaper story published in The Sydney Morning Herald, 27 February 1904, there was a report written "by a recent visitor" to New Australia in Paraguay. He recounts a meeting with Hunter Davidson saying, "He told me he preferred living on his estancia [cattle ranch] to living in town, though he owns one of the finest houses in Villa Rica." Davidson named his house in Villa Rica "Liberty Hall".

The report went on to say they climbed the tower at Captain Davidson's place and "in spite of his 70 odd years, the captain climbed the rickety stairs with the agility of a schoolboy."

This talk of the vigour of youth might account for him fathering a further 4 children with Paraguayan woman, Enriqueta Silvia Dávalos. The first was born in 1892 when Hunter was 65 years old, the last in 1899 when he was 72. There was life in the old sea dog.

In February 1896, Hunter's wife, Mary, died Baltimore, Maryland, and in 1899, just after the birth of his last child, he married Enriqueta Silvia Dávalos in Patiño Cué, Paraguay. Enriqueta was 46 years younger than Hunter and the indicator I take from that is that it makes Louisa Crossley, at only 19 years his junior, look positively aged. Does this make it any more credible that Louisa and Hunter might have had that relationship in 1871 from which Reginald Armorgie was the outcome? All I can do is to give you the clues and let you make the connections.

CAPT. HUNTER DAVIDSON.

I almost forgot to add Hunter Davidson's death at the age of 86 on 16 February 1913 in Pirayú, Paraguay. This is about 60 miles from Villa Rica and on the outskirts of Asunción, the capital of Paraguay.

HERE IS WHERE I REST MY CASE

Hunter Davidson led a life that was certainly more than ordinary but a good story doesn't just automatically make him my great great grandfather. I ask myself whether I have really just replaced the family folklore that held Spero Armorgie to be a Greek sailor with another piece of folklore that suggests he was an American sailor with Scottish roots.

I have one last piece of evidence to review, as subjective as all the others, but it's a photograph; the only existing one of my great grandfather, Reginald Armorgie. A photograph allegedly speaks a thousand words, so I have lined Reg up in an identity parade - possibly not for the first time in his existence. This time he is lined up next to my prime suspect, actually more correctly my *latest* prime suspect until I can find someone else to fit up as being my great great grandfather.

Hunter Davidson (left) and Reginald Armorgie (right).

The portrait photograph on the left was taken of Hunter Davidson in London in 1875, aged 49. I do not know the origins of Reg's photograph except that it is a most precious possession so kindly given to me by my cousin, Peter Blaney.

It is now the appropriate time to consider other Davidson descendants and see the clues that they hold that point to an apparent connection to me.

THE GOWAN CONNECTION

You will remember how I have identified 17 people to whom I was DNA matched and who also had Francis Thornton Chew as an ancestor in their family trees. You will also remember how I was knocked back when I found documents that showed I was unlikely to be related to him in spite of my faith in DNA evidence. I am therefore very cautious about having so far found DNA matches to 42 people who have ancestors who are related to Hunter Davidson, and even one who is a recent direct descendant of his; that direct descendant is Nicola Gowan. It is worth looking at her connection to Hunter Davidson as this is important when trying to decide if I have any claim to the Davidson pedigree.

True to type, I will start with supposition. I found a record of a ship, the *City of Montreal*, arriving in New York on 16 July 1872 having sailed from Liverpool via Queenstown, Ireland, and on the passenger manifest were two American passengers travelling together; a Hunter Davidson and a Mary Davidson,. The handwritten name, "Mary", is unclear but is listed as an 18 years old spinster, whilst Hunter Davidson's entry is clear and shows him listed as aged 50 and married. This particular transatlantic trip may well have been related to Hunter meeting with Dr Manuel Garcia, the Argentine Minister in London.

This ship's record doesn't exactly place this Hunter Davidson as the one I have described as my prime Spero suspect, as he would have been aged 45, neither does it identify Mary. It *could* be Hunter's eldest daughter, Leila, who was 18 at this date. It is a peripheral record but I have learned not to dismiss such records as they can hold unexpected valuable information.

Moving to the facts, you will remember Leila as the daughter after whom Hunter's Maryland Oyster Police ship was named. Was she taken on a trip with her father to Europe? If this were Leila, it would have been her first recorded visit to England, which would be significant as this would be where she ends her days many years in the future.

Leila Davidson married Dr Bowie Campbell Gowan in Maryland in 1875 and I have a record of her and Bowie living with Bowie's sister in Kensington, London, on the 1881 census, with their two young sons. They had previously been in Sydney, Australia, in the period between marriage in Maryland and living in Kensington, as their son, Hyde Clarendon Gowan, was born in Sydney in 1878.

This has little bearing on my life other than Hyde Clarendon Gowan is Nicola Gowan's grandfather, and I am shown as DNA matched to Nicola. The question for me is whether Hunter Davidson is our shared ancestor? As previously, I'll give you the clue and you choose whether you make the connection. I would urge a different consideration because, amongst all the other preceding Davidson conjecture, a DNA connection is hard evidence of a relationship. The only bit in question is whether I am related to Nicola Gowan through the Davidson line or some other family line. I can find no other family lines in Nicola's family tree to which I have any other evidence of connection to, only the Davidson link.

As a supplementary yet irrelevant piece of information, other than perhaps proving the theory of six degrees of separation, I found that I have a DNA match to a Mike Smith in Wellington, New Zealand, and Mike is the ex-husband of Nicola Gowan's sister, Carol Gowan. I am almost certainly related to Mike through my paternal grandmother who lived in the same area of north Wales as Mike's paternal grandmother. Small world - or *byd bach* as they might say in those parts if they used Google translate.

Special thanks go to Carol Gowan for sharing a lot of the Gowan / Davidson family research that her father had done in the days before the internet. I take my hat off to James Hyde Bowie Gowan for his dedication to his search – if I had been him, I'd have waited for the internet to be invented.

THE CHERYL PICCOLA-SULLIVAN CONNECTION

This was a tricky one but it turned out to be very revealing. I had an identified DNA match to Cheryl Piccola-Sullivan of the same strength of connection as I do to Nicola Gowan. What I didn't have was any family tree for Cheryl and therefore, initially, no idea who our shared ancestor might be. My efforts to contact Cheryl via the DNA website have been unsuccessful so I have had to channel my inner DNA detective, or gene genie.

I found that Cheryl lives in Las Vegas - the famous one in Nevada, not the less famous one, more local to me; *Higgitt's Las Vegas Amusements and £1 Burger Bar* in Blackpool, Lancashire. The fact that Cheryl had been married to men with surnames Piccola, Sullivan and Argo very much masked my ability to find a lead on where she was born and her birth name, so that I could work back to her parents, grandparents and so on. My breakthrough came when I found a cemetery record for Joann Davidson in 2013. Joann was born Barbara Joann Parks and I found a record of her marriage to Archie Hamilton Davidson. I also found an online obituary for Cheryl's sister, Cathy who died, in 2008 that corroborated the identity of Cheryl and Cathy's parents. I was interested; of course I was.

COLIN ARMORGIE

I pieced it all together and found that Cheryl was born Cheryl Ann Davidson in Rockmart, Georgia, USA in 1955. Her paternal line goes back in a straight ascendency to Archer Allen Davidson. Archer was Hunter Davidson's uncle. This, I think, is another strong clue that I will leave with you to make any connection you choose.

THE PABLO TABACHNIK CONNECTION

If finding a connection to Cheryl was tricky then my apparent connection to Pablo Tabachnik was, and remains, more frustrating than tricky to establish. If evidence were ever required, my apparent connection to Pablo just gives me the opportunity to further prove that old adage that it is indeed a small world in which we live - or *mundo pequeño* as they might say in Buenos Aires if they used Google translate.

I have managed to trace the descendants of Ruben Osvaldo Davidson Dávalos, the oldest of Hunter Davidson's children with his second wife, Enriqueta, born on 25 October 1892 in Villa Rica, Paraguay. Ruben, who died on 10 September 1966, had a granddaughter, Maria de las Mercedes Davidson Meade Monje, and not only is that a great name but a name that she must have got fed up of being asked to spell. She possibly heard this question quite a lot:

"De dónde viene, chiquita?"

"Cuánto tiempo tienes?" could have been the well-worn response.

This translates roughly as, "It could be worse, I suppose; I could be called Armorgie."

COLIN ARMORGIE

Hey, every day is a school day.

Maria married Roberto Tabachnik, a lawyer in San Juan, Argentina. Roberto is from a Polish family who immigrated to Argentina before WWI. They have 2 sons, Gustavo and Pablo, and carry on the family tradition of having a big internet presence. Pablo is an Argentinian legend who has been a professional table tennis player who has represented Argentina at 3 Olympic Games.

Maybe the title of this book should have been the less-than-snappy, *From Leamington Spa to Argentinian Ping Pong in One Giant Leap*? Yes, admittedly it needs a bit of work so leave it with me.

My frustration comes from having tried to contact Pablo and Roberto Tabachnik but without success. My emails keep getting bounced as perceived attempts at phishing, which is kind of true but not proper Nigerian Prince kind-of-true. If (ha!) I could get a DNA sample from either of them, that would reveal the crock of gold at the end of my rainbow, and I could remove the phrase about me giving the clues and you making the connections. In fact, crock of gold doesn't really cover it; it would be like the person in the quiet coach of the train turning off their mobile phone (you know who you are), combined with the person in the seat in front of me on the plane putting their seat in the upright position for the whole flight (you know who I am), and Shelley learning how to clean hair out of the shower plughole so that I didn't have to feel like Mrs Chewbacca's gynaecologist every time I did it. Anyway, that's sufficient of my OCD revelations for now but a flavour of how much it would mean to me.

A man can dream when he calms down a bit.

AN UNCOMFORTABLE TRUTH

I may be guilty of supposition, I may guilty of conjecture, I may even have trodden on the toes of conspiracy, but I very much don't want to have to make a front page retraction on a red top, declaring large, "WE LIED". Liverpool will understand.

All of what I have written has been written in good faith and, as much as I dearly want it to be true, I cannot guarantee it. If I really wanted to provide you with a guarantee, I would give it to you in a box labelled "pop-up toaster". I won't even use the word "honestly" because that would just sound disingenuous.

In the way that some in my family have inherited ginger hair and the Jackson Gully[18], there is no point in delving into any family's history if you don't want to find an uncomfortable truth - or many uncomfortable truths. Yes, I could have kept to myself the things that I have found, or maybe have whispered them quietly in discreet family gatherings, but with me rarely heeding good advice, I had a

---

[18] A very wide hair parting inherited from my mother's family and often wrongly mistaken for a receding hairline in the males. It's not balding, honestly it's not; I can guarantee it. Have a look at the photo of Hunter Davidson for an illustration. Oh, hang on...

better idea; I'll tell the world in a book! Great idea? We'll see.

My mother's recollection of an air-brushed version of her family history, related by word of mouth, is the modern day equivalent of social media postings where everyone else's life can appear to be so perfect and make your own life appear mundane at best. The Prozac Deceit is not for me.

There is a well-worn saying that you can't choose your relatives, however, I have been blessed with an opportunity to choose mine. Not knowing the true identity of Spero Armorgie, nominally my great great grandfather, I could have chosen anyone, I could have made up any story about the origin of my surname using some corny Latin anagram device. I realise that I may not have always made the best choices in life but I will stand by what I have written here.

Having written this story it raises many questions but there are 3 fundamental questions to which I still can't find answers that I am totally comfortable with. I will explain here but not in the cause of seeking answers, just to make others aware that I am not blind to the sensitivities of others.

First, should I take my mother's family approach and bury any suggestions about my heritage being possibly tainted with connections that could be felt to be unpalatable? I have written my own history and have connected my family to real events and real people, but disconnecting my family wouldn't change those events. If I say it is raining today, you could go and check but you are not going to make it stop raining by closing the curtains.

My second question is the moral judgement of whether I should be making connections between my family and the families of other named people. My DNA test results connect me incontrovertibly to many people, alive and dead, but the question is whether I should go as far as to call out which one of their ancestors they share with me and make suggestions about the circumstances of that connection?

My level of personal difficulty ramps up in my third question. This is consideration of whether what I have written is going to sit comfortably with my wider Armorgie family? And I think this extends to the dead as well as the living, as I still feel a responsibility to the memories of those who have gone. Without me making any subjective judgement, I can say that I have come to terms with what I have found in my search for Spero - but I realise that this isn't all about me. Yes, it might read like it's all about me, the perks of writing your own book, but I do not overlook the fact that *my* family history is actually the family history of all *other* family members. Each one of those family members will individually and undoubtedly feel differently.

All I can do is to say that it has never my intention to offend anyone or to tarnish the memories of ancestors, moreover, I would highlight that the Armorgie history is full of facts about which we should be interested and even proud. I guess it's not the facts that are making me ask this third question, rather it is the elements of conjecture that I have introduced. Yes, I could have omitted those but I fall back into a comfortable place and draw upon the sayings of those far wiser than me.

French philosopher Claude Lévi-Strauss once stated that, "*The scientist is not a person who gives the right answers, he is one who asks the right questions.*"

Hopefully I have asked the right questions rather than provided the wrong answers.

A BIG FAT MIDDLE, TWO ENDS AND SEVERAL BEGINNINGS

I look back at how I have told Spero's story and can say that it *did* have a beginning, a middle and an end – but not necessarily in that order and not necessarily just one of each. Maybe it's just been my experience but I found it quite hard to tell my family history story in chronological order. I could have made it a very linear story but the thing that makes Spero's story interesting is how I had to discover all the elements before I could piece them together and tell it. In a rather rewarding way, the story became about the lives of real people and the times through which they lived. It also became about me in a way that I never expected.

As a piece of unashamed literary conceit, I can draw a parallel with Hamlet, the family history story about a bloke who was the King of Denmark, allegedly. Spero's story started "*in medias res*", as the Romans would call it, opening in the midst of the plot. It is also like Hamlet in as much as it focussed more on the *characters* than the action. OK, a minor point, so what if I haven't actually read Hamlet? I've seen some Hollywood adaptations which are sufficient for my blinkered needs. Hey, I might as well be hanged for a sheep as a lamb.

COLIN ARMORGIE

In reality though, Spero's story has turned out to be more of a story of part of *my* life in a very cathartic way.

PITHY QUOTES RECONSIDERED

It is understandable that family gatherings for reunions or funerals usually spark discussions about family history. There is an assumption, at least on my part, that someone else must know more than me. The reality is that everyone knows a little, usually the same little as everyone else knows, and some know more than others. Perhaps more dangerous is the person who is hailed by others as the family oracle, someone believed to have communication with the God of All Things Armorgie.

It is at this point that I give a gullibility warning:

"In the country of the blind, the one-eyed man is king."

I hope that others find my story as fascinating as I have found it, but please heed what I have said about my father's tendency to embellishment and my mother's blind faith in everything she was told. I may not just have inherited the Jackson Gully.

You know I started by saying I had no pithy quotes? They kind of found me as I researched and so I liberally dispersed them through the story to pad it out in way that may have tarnished my already tainted believability. For the unbelievers I will even draw on the Bible as a source of wisdom and urge you to take heed of the warning in Matthew 15:14 that states:

COLIN ARMORGIE

"If a blind man leads a blind man, both will fall into a pit."

If you fall into that pit, you'll be on your own and I won't have pushed you. Oh, if you see me in the pit, please help me out – always assuming that we are not in the country of the blind and you can actually see me. To tie myself in knots I sometimes manage.

Oh, talking of needing help, if you see me in the libel courts, you'll know how the next book in the series will start but, with luck, it should boost the sales of the remaining copies of this book. Well, at least the copies that manage to escape being shredded by court order.

If You Could See Your Ancestors
By Nellie Winslow Simmons Randall

If you could see your ancestors
All standing in a row,
Would you be proud of them or not?
Or don't you really know?

Some strange discoveries are made
In climbing family trees.
And some of them, you know,
Do not particularly please.

If you could see your ancestors
All standing in a row,
There might be some of them perhaps
You shouldn't care to know.

But here's another question
Which requires a different view
If you could "meet" your ancestors
Would they be proud of you?

WHAT HAS ALL THIS GIVEN ME?

In fact, what actually is "all this" that I've been given? I've kind of lost sight, so let me draw it back in and ask simply whether I have identified Spero?

It is difficult to answer this categorically as it comes back to what I was saying about asking the right questions. The logical and superficial answer is that, no, I haven't identified Spero – but I feel like I have *found* him. You should have realised by now that I changed my criteria for completion. I started out being guided by my head but ended up finding more answers in my heart. My feeling of achievement is immense, and it has consumed me in terms of time, money, emotion and loss of sleep. Better than that, I have enjoyed every minute.

Up to now I had only *verbally* bored so many people with my story, perhaps with the odd PowerPoint presentation thrown in, but I am thankful that I found sufficient motivation to write a book about it to maximise that effect.

I have reached a point where, in a way, I don't feel that I need to find the real name of the man who called himself Spero Armorgie. If I am honest with myself, the quest (I nearly said journey) has been so fulfilling, to find a name could mean it is over - and why would I want something that has been so satisfying to end?

COLIN ARMORGIE

I will have to start procrastinating to prolong the satisfaction. I'll start tomorrow.

Writing this *has* given me answers; I now have the answer to the "where does that name come from?" question. OK, more correctly, I have **an** answer but however I tell it, it will be the same story – just a *little* bit longer in print than the verbal summary. The verbal version, however, doesn't leave the opportunity for royalties, so you better get comfortable with the print version.

Man has an inherent need to understand and my need went further than just blindly accepting Greece as the answer. I still may not know the truth but I know as much as there is to know for now, as well as extending this with my own 'truth'; a truth that I can cling on to. It may be sacrilegious to say this, but on the basis that I've probably already unintentionally upset so many people, documenting my own truth was following the way that the ancients explained away in religious texts those things they had no other explanation for.

Writing this has also given me the answer to why it took me so long to realise that Spero Armorgie was probably not the name of my great-great-grandfather? I suspect it was because I had to prove beyond reasonable doubt that there was no evidence to support the existence of this as a name that anyone had ever gone by – other than for the purposes of formalising just two documents in 1871. Oh, and now a third document; the one you are reading.

When I say "prove beyond reasonable doubt", it didn't mean that I had to prove anything to be statistically significant. In truth it was about my need to prove Spero Armorgie's phantom persona credentials to myself in a way that I was happy with. More than that, and going deeper into my psyche, I think I still had that need to want to impress my parents, particularly my father. Both my parents are dead, but not in spirit. I think my father, who was a

AMERICA'S HOPE

Liverpudlian by birth and Sarkese by choice, had that same particular deep seated need as me to want to understand his heritage. His stories and joking about it were likely just a cover for his disappointment of not knowing and not being able to find out. That's what can be so hard – not knowing *and* not having had the opportunities to find out.

My father led an increasingly tortured life, right up until his death. To the outside world he was all *bonhomie*, the life and soul of the party, sociable and engaging. In private, and he was a very private man, he harboured demons and insecurities that ultimately consumed him. He was not tortured by the trivia of not knowing the origins of his surname; I think his torment was bigger ticket, him feeling he hadn't cleared the bar of what he deemed to be success, or rather he kept pushing the bar higher each time he got close. The reality of his life was the absolute achievement of success in so many areas, which was clear for everyone to see except himself.

The first of the many things of value he gave me in my life was the name Armorgie. His father, my grandfather, was for many years the sole surviving Armorgie male anywhere, and was therefore solely responsible for passing on the name without which you wouldn't be reading this. Near the time of Grampy's death, he was being sustained with oxygen and he wheezed a prophetic prediction to my Dad. At that time, Mum and Dad's family was a work-in-progress and they had 3 of their eventual 4 sons. Grampy, who realised that his hours were numbered, let alone his days, jokingly warned my Dad that he was in danger of making the name Armorgie as common as Smith.

In me telling the story in this book, following my Dad's tradition of adding theories and embellishments, bells and whistles, I hope to feel the hand of my father on my shoulder and feel his soul a little less troubled.

Hope has been a theme; I hold that thought.

TYING UP LOOSE THREADS

I started off lost, remember, so it feels right to question whether I ultimately did find my way to my destination. Have I found Spero, the man who was my great-great-grandfather? Actually, these are two different questions with different answers; one question easier than the other answer.

The easier of those two questions to answer is that I have certainly found my way to *a* destination, perhaps not really **the** place I expected to end up and, hopefully, not the final destination. I can't blame anyone for giving me poor directions nor for failing to give me directions at all because I pissed them all off (and continue to split infinitives despite Mrs Davies' break time tutelage. She probably wouldn't have approved of the profanity either.) I will shoulder that blame. I now realise that the destination is not always important as I have gained so much else along the way. I now understand myself better and I now understand what things are important to me.

The difficult question is whether I have found Spero? I previously mentioned "probability" and I know how I feel but you kind of realised that I copped out and asked you to make your connection from the clues to the truth. Talking of *kopping out*, when I said that Liverpudlians would likely see me as a southerner you can now understand why this might be; I could be a southerner or a Southerner or both.

I am convinced that in my research and building a database of over 12,000 persons of interest from my DNA connections that I will very likely have seen the name of the man who called himself Spero. The possible corollary of that is that I have found *so many* names that I now fear I can't see the wood for the trees. Life was easier when Spero was a simple Greek sailor.

It would be understandable that a man coming from the likely background of having lived through a civil war, keeping a secret was probably more a survival technique he had acquired rather than just a device for simply preventing a scandal. Maybe I should respect that and not go seeking his identity? Yeah, right.

I will also return to the scene of my initial disclaimer and ask again that this book is not judged on the sole basis of the facts that it contains. Your honour, I can't stress enough that the history I have recounted here has just been my personal telling of a story, a whole story and nothing but a story. It is mine, all mine and nothing but mine. If others had told it, unlike me they would certainly have included bits of scurrilous accusation, tittle-tattle, innuendo and they would have told it differently. I will emphasise that there is no definitive identification of Spero Armorgie as such, so maybe this whole thing should be called *"The Colin Armorgie Chronicle"*?

I will make one final polite request, a plea bargain if you like, to those people who might recognise in my story a relative that they could share with me. Spit into a test tube for me, please – we need to know.

THE FINAL CHAPTER OR THE NEXT CHAPTER?

A family history story really has no end but I will be merciful and bring this story to an end. It is only this part of the story that ends because history doesn't have an end. As I type this, it is current; as you read it, it is already history.

In the same way that I have over-used literary metaphors to tell my story, I thought I would draw a quote from the book and film with a name that sums up not having a conclusion: *The Neverending Story*. The first reference I found to the film was a warning that the "content that may disturb children". And so the quote was found.

I previously said that *my* search for Spero would be time limited; it's in here somewhere but I can't remember where. Other Armorgies, I hope, will become curious in time and seek more, and will continue the search. The only problem is that nostalgia is the preserve of the elderly, so their time has yet to come. If you are one of the young, then congratulations; you'll understand one day and remember these words when nostalgia finally grips you. While you are waiting for that hand to grip, let me presume to offer some more unsolicited advice: Don't wait until it is too late to ask the family elders about *their* lives. One day you'll *want* to know and it may be too late, as I may have found to my cost. And don't devolve the responsibility to Instagram because my generation largely avoided that.

The bit of family history that I think I failed to identify the importance of in my youth, is what is particularly seen in Nordic culture as sagas; the oral history passed from one generation to the next. Even if you end up hearing the family history from your parents, they will typically have at least 140 years of stories. That is, their three score years and ten and the three score years and ten that their parents told them about. Spero Armorgie appeared (and disappeared) in my timeline 141 years before my parents died. Damn!

Finally, for those Armorgies still in the stage of their lives when they are more content to make history rather than research it, make it as memorable and dramatic as you can – but, please, make a record of it and spare some poor, future descendant the pain of having to unravel another bloody family mystery!

REFERENCES

Just one point of reference is needed here and this is it:

Throughout my life, when I wasn't participating in the business of enjoying myself, I spent large chunks of my life writing technical documents and academic essays. In those works to which I put my name, every source of information had to be referenced and foul language definitely had to be absent. I very much didn't feel the need to perpetuate that here and have to give references; the shackles were off.

I did find through experience, however, that foul language could actually bring success and engender support for my cause; I used it to help me win the world queue jumping championship and get everyone behind me. I have used it here, you will have noticed.

If you've actually read this story you will know where and how I found my sources information, and for the bits that I couldn't find, I gave a reasoned hypothesis. I am the author of my own family history and the real source is in my heart. Simon Schama, suck that up, analyse it and make a documentary for BBC2.

ABOUT THE AUTHOR

In a way, this is the hardest chapter to write - Colin Armorgie gets to write about Colin Armorgie and has to keep it brief and snappy whilst being informative and not digressing any further. Let's face it, that ain't going to happen, is it? If it were brief and snappy it would have been on the back cover to put off people from buying this book.

In 1957, Prime Minister Harold Macmillan, declared that Britons had "never had it so good", which was prophetic as my parents were blessed with my arrival in this world in that year. The county of Cheshire is where I began a nomadic existence that soon took me to schooling and living in various locations in the Gin and Jag Belt of Surrey and Sussex.

Studying geography at University College London prepared me in part for writing this book but I had to first get 40 years of working life out of the way.

Like the early American pioneers, at some point I headed west; in my case, down the M4 motorway, hanging a right down the A417 at Swindon to settle for a short sojourn in the city of Gloucester. Thence southbound on the M5 to my current home in Frampton Cotterell, near Bristol, which is also serendipitously very close to ground zero for the Armorgie name in the city of Bath.

I ceased working for a living in 2019 and easily separated the living from the working. I became the self-appointed investigator and documenter of the Armorgie family history – but you should know that if you have actually read the book. If you are idly thumbing through someone else's copy of this book and have yet to read it, please don't be put off by this little autobiography. You would never have watched *Jaws* had you simply read, "Smalltown police chief overcomes fear of water by unconventional means."

If you have still to decide, or if you have liked what you have just read, please read one of the other selected short publications by the author, selected from a long list of two:

- Ball, D.J. and Armorgie, C.J. 1980: Fuel-use and SO2 emissions in central London in 1978/79. GLC Research Memorandum RM566.
- Schwar, M. J., Moorcroft, J. S., Laxen, D. P., Thompson, M., & Armorgie, C. (1988). Baseline metal-in-dust concentrations in Greater London. Science of the Total Environment, 68, 25–43.

These publications may not still be available in all good booksellers but the references just go to show that you can rely on scientists to spell your name correctly even if their subject matter has a somewhat niche appeal. Oh, and before you ask, no, I don't know what happened in the fallow years between 1988 and 2023; writers' block, I guess.

That autobiography wasn't so hard to write after all; the reading of it may be the bigger challenge[19].

---

[19] This is the final annoying footnote, honestly.

Printed in Great Britain
by Amazon